100 IDEAS FOR SUPPORTING PUPILS WITH DYSPRAXIA AND DCD

Amanda Kirby and Lynne Peters

continuum

Continuum International Publishing Group

The Tower Building	80 Maiden Lane
11 York Road	Suite 704
SE1 7NX	New York, NY 10038

www.continuumbooks.com

British Library Cataloguing-in-Publication Data
A catalogue record for this book is available from the British
Library.

ISBN: 08264 94404   (paperback)

Library of Congress Cataloging-in-Publication Data
Kirby, Amanda. Peters, Lynne
   100 ideas for supporting pupils with dyspraxia and DCD /
Amanda Kirby and Lynne Peters.
      p. cm. -- (Continuum one hundreds series)
    ISBN-13: 978-0-8264-9440-5 (pbk.)
    ISBN-10: 0-8264-9440-4 (pbk.)
   1. Children with disabilities--Education. 2. Movement disorders
in children. 3. Apraxia. 4. Motor ability in children. I. Peters,
Lynne. II. Title. III. Title: One hundred ideas for supporting pupils
with dyspraxia and DCD. IV. Title: Hundred ideas for supporting
pupils with dyspraxia and DCD. V. Series.

   LC4015.K47 2007
   371.9'16--dc22

2006029550

Typeset by Ben Cracknell Studios | www.benstudios.co.uk
Printed and bound in Great Britain by Ashford Colour Press,
Gosport, Hampshire

CONTENTS

SECTION 3 Secondary school

This book has been written to give ideas and tips for supporting children and young people with developmental coordination disorder (DCD) and dyspraxia. However, many of the ideas will be useful for all children in the class, with and without motor coordination difficulties.

The book has been divided into sections relating to pre-school, primary and secondary school. Some of the themes are repeated and further graded as the child moves through school. If the child lacks skills in a particular area, consider looking at a younger age section. The tips and ideas are set at a developmental level and it is important to ensure first that the necessary foundation skills are in place, such as the pre-writing skills or basic skills required to use scissors. All the activities are safe to use with all children within the school setting.

Children with movement difficulties can vary greatly and may not just appear 'clumsy'. In the class, for example, they may bump into things, drop books or trip over, but often present with other symptoms and signs such as inattention and fidgetiness. In the school day the child may have difficulties in other areas and in specific subjects like mathematics, literacy or PE. Typical difficulties may include recording information, organizing work, copying work down from the board, playing with puzzles, coordination in PE and self-care.

Providing early intervention for individuals with coordination difficulties will help promote positive self-esteem and encourage social interaction with others.

When talking about 'hot spots' in this book we are referring to those areas in the school where there may be potential problems for the child or times in the day when they may have greater difficulties than their peers.

We will refer to the child as 'him' or 'he' throughout the book for consistency. Three times as many boys as girls have DCD. However, similar approaches to those shown can be used with girls, and gender-specific advice is included in the book where appropriate.

The terms DCD and dyspraxia have been used interchangeably for the purpose of the book. For more information on the disorder itself refer to the additional recommended reading and websites in the appendix.

Pre-school

STARTING THE DAY

Most pre-school children with coordination difficulties would not usually have a diagnosis of dyspraxia/DCD as it is more difficult to distinguish between DCD and developmental delay at this stage. Some children's motor skills will improve as they have greater opportunities to explore their environment. Therefore, in the early years the activities detailed are more generic and should be set at a developmentally appropriate level.

Starting at school or nursery can be a traumatic experience for some children. Some may settle in very quickly, while others may appear scared or frightened by the ordeal. Children with DCD may find it harder to adapt to changes in their daily routine or may present with skills at a level of a younger child.

The day should be explained to the child in advance so he knows what to expect. Take time to reassure him that his parents will be collecting him at the end of the session.

It's often helpful to provide the child with a visual timetable or story board showing what will happen when he arrives, who will be there to meet him and when he will have a drink and something to eat (see Idea 17 to find out how to make a story board).

Showing the child where the toilets are and letting him know that he can use them whenever he needs to is especially reassuring. This is particularly important for the child with DCD as he may need to go to the toilet in a rush and may have poor bladder control. He may ask to go more often because of anxiety as well as need.

The child with DCD may experience difficulty with toilet training and be later developing these skills than his peers.

Bottom-wiping may be particularly tricky to do. This may be because the child does not have the ability to balance while sitting on the toilet and is not able to take his hand behind him to wipe. He may also not be aware of where his bottom is to wipe!

Make sure there is toilet paper near to the child so he can reach out while sitting on the toilet (provide wet wipes or toilet wipes to help the child to clean better). To improve balance for bottom-wiping, ensure that both feet are placed firmly on the floor, providing the child with a stable base. If this is not possible, provide a step for the child to place his feet on. Telephone books bound together can be useful for this. Having a hand rail to hold will provide stability.

The child should be able to reach behind his body and under his legs in order to bottom-wipe. To help with this, try getting the child to pass a small ball or balloon around the legs in a figure of eight. Then get him to pass the ball or balloon around his body, changing it from one hand to the other. You could also stick stickers on different places on the child's body – front and back – and get him to find the stickers.

It's worth having a word with the parents and suggesting that buttons and zips are best kept to a minimum. Ask them to provide a spare pair of pants in case of accidents.

Make sure you have regular toilet times to get the child into a routine, such as every break and lunchtime.

COPING WITH TOILETS AND TOILETING

Children with poor coordination often have difficulty managing eating and drinking utensils. They may have problems using both hands together, a weak grasp and poor control when using the utensils in a specific order to perform a range of tasks.

Look at the type of cup the child is using. A soft paper cup can be squeezed too hard, causing the contents to spill over, and can be difficult to hold. Choose a rigid cup with a weighted base. Make sure it has a good size handle so that the child can get all his fingers in the hole, giving him a better grip.

Consider where the child is having his drink. Is he sitting in a stable position? If he is sitting on the floor, is he supported by a wall as this will provide extra stability? If he is sitting at a table, are his feet on the floor providing adequate support and is the table at about waist height? Too high a table will mean the child cannot get sufficient balance to take his hands away from his body and drink from the cup.

Does the child have to carry the cup across a busy classroom where other children are playing or walking? This may end in the child bumping into another child or the furniture and spilling the drink, which may cause distress. Place the drink on the table where the child is sitting and make sure the cup is not overly full.

The child with DCD is often later learning to ride a bike than his peers. In some cases the child never masters the art of riding a bike or scooter and gives up in frustration. This can prove socially challenging when other children are participating in outdoor play, as the child may feel more isolated from the children who are able to ride successfully.

Consider starting off with a tricycle or scooter as this may be easier to use to practise pedalling skills. A scooter allows the child to push off and not have to worry about pedalling. Get the child to push off consistently with the same foot. A pedal car or go-kart can be easier to use as the child is in a stable sitting position and can learn the art of pedalling before moving on to balancing and pedalling at the same time. Make sure he can reach the pedals easily, and consider using elbow and knee pads, even with a scooter. Choose a scooter with a large enough platform, so that the child can easily place his feet on it.

OUTDOOR PLAY ON TRICYCLES AND SCOOTERS

OUTDOOR PLAY ON BIKES

In order to ride a bike successfully the child will need to acquire and combine several different skills:

○ Coordination
○ Balance
○ Spatial awareness.

SAFETY

First prepare the child for riding the bicycle. Make sure he wears a suitable sized helmet. Elbow and knee pads are useful to minimize bumps and bruises and give confidence as the child may be more likely to fall off or fear falling. Gloves are also essential to prevent abrasion to the palms in the event of a fall.

BALANCE

The bicycle must be small enough so that the child can place both feet flat on the ground when the saddle has been adjusted all the way down. This will provide the child with a safe stopping mechanism and make him feel more secure. Stabilizers often act to destabilize the child, so it is better to lower the seat of the bicycle.

It's often a good idea to take off the pedals and get the child to move the bicycle using his feet so that he can get used to the feeling of movement. Make sure he pushes off each time with the same foot.

Talk to the child and involve him in how he thinks he can improve his technique – what does he think he could do better, such as push off harder, pedal faster, watch where he is going? It's important to get the child to give this verbal feedback and to involve him in the learning process.

Mark out the playground with a path to follow, so that all children go in the same direction. This will prevent them bumping into each other and will be one less thing for the child to be concerned about.

Children often have difficulty sustaining a sitting position on the floor without support and will quite often get into a position themselves where they can get support, i.e. close to a wall or table, or they may lean against other children when sitting on the floor. In addition, the child with movement difficulties may also appear inattentive and fidgety if he is uncomfortable. The child with DCD may also have additional overlapping difficulties with attention deficit disorder which may present with difficulties in maintaining attention.

Make story time as interactive as possible, using props to involve the children, such as puppets and large story books. Allow the children to have movement breaks and limit the time they are sitting on the floor. If the child is very fidgety give him a 'fiddle toy'. This could be a soft ball or a small toy that the child brings in with him from home.

Ensuring that the child is sitting in a good position facing the teacher will keep him focused on the story and allow the teacher to bring him back into focus if his concentration drifts. You could think about using small chairs for the children to sit on, instead of sitting on the floor, if the session is any longer than a few minutes.

Allow a variety of sitting positions for the whole class and let them choose how they want to sit.

IDEA 7

Young children with DCD may appear fidgety and have difficulties listening and staying on task. Encouraging them to 'tune in' at this stage is helpful preparation for starting at primary school.

Sit beside the child and first engage him in parallel play. Begin to extend the child's play by demonstration, without interfering in what he is doing. He may respond in one of the following ways:

○ He may not appear to notice, but begin to imitate your actions.
○ He may stop his play and watch you with interest.
○ He may destroy your game!

Call the child's name, establish eye contact and deliver a short, simple instruction. Then gain the child's attention while he is actively engaged in the task. Call his name, say 'look', 'listen', but don't give any instruction until you have established eye contact again. Instructions must be related to the task you are asking him to do. Keep them very short to begin with, for example, 'Copy me', 'Do this'. Remember to accompany them with appropriate gestures.

Slowly teach the child to listen and take in what you say without stopping what he is doing. Praise him when he is attending. You could also use a timer to show how long a task will take.

Painting activities can improve motor control but may be hard for the child with DCD. Practice needs to be undertaken on a regular basis, for example, ten minutes of some of the following tasks, three times a week, will help the child to improve his fine motor coordination.

It is important to make sure the tools are appropriate so the child can participate adequately. Larger handled tools help the child to adopt a better grip and allow him to manipulate the tool better when completing any activity.

Changing the position of the child or the activity may make it easier or harder for the child to complete his work. When painting, place paper on the wall or on an easel and have the child stand to paint. Alternatively, lower the easel so the child can sit on a chair. Another position could be placing the paper on the floor and allowing the child to lie in a prone position (on his stomach) or to kneel. This will also strengthen back and neck muscles. Lowering the easel could allow the child to 'high kneel' to paint.

Some children with DCD may not like to touch certain textures. The child may try to avoid the activity completely; for example, if he is made to do finger painting he may report that he feels sick when he has to put his hands into wet paint! If this is the case, try making pictures or doing activities avoiding fingers and using brushes or starting with 'semi-dry' materials such as pasta shapes or dough. Helping the child to overcome touching particular textures can also be achieved by making hide and seek games. For example, put objects in a bag of dried pasta shapes or polystyrene packing material, get the child to find the object without looking and then ask him to describe it. Other semi-solid materials such as jelly could also be introduced.

With any activity involving water or sand play the equipment should have big handles to make it easier to grip. Use language as well as movement to help the child reinforce what he is seeing and feeling.

Start with the child making big shapes in wet sand placed in a tray. Encourage the child to talk about the shapes he is making in the sand as this may be a route to preparing for writing skills at a later date. You could also hide objects in the sand and ask the child to find a specific shape. Then you can have a discussion about shape, form and texture. Get the child to talk about what he is touching by asking questions such as, 'Is it smooth or rough?'

Try getting the child to blow bubbles in a bowl of water. Dye the water with food dye and get the child to squeeze a sponge in the water and press the water out onto a large sheet of paper to make different patterns. This helps fine motor skills. Different sized containers or jugs can be introduced for pouring the water back and forward. Also use sand and a sieve and encourage the child to talk about what is happening and what he can see. These activities help to develop muscle strength and coordination.

The child with DCD may avoid playing with jigsaws and construction toys. There are many different reasons for this. The child may:

o have visual perceptual difficulties and not see the pieces as clearly as other children
o be unable to orientate the pieces appropriately
o have a poor grip and poor fine motor control
o not have had the practice he needs to master the activity and has learnt to avoid those sorts of toys at home.

Consider where the child is completing these activities as he may need a quiet place in order to concentrate. He may be more sensitive to noise, and additional distractions may be enough to encourage him to be diverted away to another activity.

Start by using small numbers of larger jigsaw pieces with clear bold colours and little pattern. Jigsaws with chunky grips on them make it easier for the child to hold, and one within a frame is good as the pieces don't move around as much. Large floor jigsaws are great to work with and also help the child to strengthen their upper body if they work in a prone position (on the stomach).

Try providing a jigsaw that is partially completed so that the child has just a few pieces to put in and can see an end in sight. This will boost his self-esteem and give him a feeling of success. Also, jigsaws that match the picture to the shape are easier for the child to see than those cut to odd shapes. And if you can find one which has a picture of the human body this can help the child to learn where body parts are. It will also help with skills such as bottom-wiping and dressing.

Try making your own jigsaw puzzles by cutting up old birthday or Christmas cards then putting them back together. Young children really enjoy these. There are computer programs available where you can make your own puzzles, such as *Puzzle Maker* from www.egames. com/ There are often free downloads where you can try these games.

JIGSAWS AND CONSTRUCTION TOYS

11

With construction toys, textured toys such as stickle bricks and 'Popoids' are easier to use than Lego and they also connect with and separate from one another more easily. Use different colours so the child can see a difference in shape. Magnetic shapes and puzzles that connect may also be easier for the child to link as they do not need as much pressure.

Visual perception is the way we interpret what is seen around us. It requires the child to be able to pick out objects from a background and memorize and hold pictures or words in the mind (visual memory). The child with DCD often has difficulties in this area which, if not helped, may later impact on writing, copying tasks and playing sports.

Matching games are a good way of helping with this. Teach simple activities such as matching shape, colour and size and identifying the odd one out. Ask the child to look around the classroom and match, for example, some of the round-shaped objects he can spot. Use everyday objects, such as farm animals, cutlery, pairs of socks or other clothing items, and get the child to match them together.

Games such as dominoes are also helpful. Start by using dominoes with pictures and then move on to using ones with spots once the child is confident with the picture dominoes. Card games such as Snap or Lotto, or simple pictorial Bingo, where the child has to match the items on the card, are also good and help to improve visual memory.

Start playing simple tracking games – create a card with a line like a snake and get the child to follow with his finger from the start of the snake's head to the tail, staying on the trail. Dot-to-dot books also help to practise tracking and following.

Where's Wally? or similar books where objects or people need to be found in a picture can be useful to work through. Encourage the child to look at the picture, scanning from left to right. If the picture is too complex try covering the page so only a segment is showing.

Alternatively, try presenting the child with three objects that look the same except for one that is placed in a different orientation, for example, on its end, upside down, on its side. Get the child to spot the difference.

IDEA

12

The child with DCD may have some difficulties visualizing objects, for example, shapes and letters. This has an effect on a number of tasks in the classroom, such as copying words from the board. Try playing some simple games to help improve the child's visual memory.

Place a number of different objects on a tray and allow the child to look at them for a short while. Then ask him to try and remember what they are, cover the tray and remove one object. Ask the child if he can see which object has been removed. Start with three objects and increase the number according to the child's ability.

A variation on this is to ask the child to spot the difference. Allow the child to see the objects on the tray to start with, then he closes his eyes and looks again after you have changed something, such as turned a doll over on its back or placed a toy car on its side.

Another good memory game is to show a shape or object to the child and then hide it. The child then has to find other objects around the room that are similar. In order to do this, he has to 'hold' the shape in his head.

Early play activities, such as manipulating toys and objects, help to develop fine motor coordination. Good hand function requires a stable trunk so the arms and hands can move freely away from the body, therefore activities which develop trunk muscles can also improve fine motor skills, such as scissor skills, pencil control and using and manipulating small toys like Lego.

Before starting any activity ensure that the child has a good sitting position. Look out for signs of poor trunk stability, such as sitting in a 'W' position (placing his bottom between his legs on the floor). If the child does this, encourage him to sit cross-legged and lean against a wall if necessary. Some children may 'flop' over on the table and prop their heads up with their hands – a chair with good support is essential before the child can begin to work freely and confidently with his hands.

Activities which promote good hand strength and skill are often found in everyday tasks such as pushing the wheelbarrow in the garden, sorting out the nuts and bolts in the shed, rolling out pastry or kneading dough to make bread.

General tasks, such as carrying, pushing, pulling things like boxes, blocks, play toys, wagons, carts, dolls' buggies, are excellent natural muscle-building activities. Put added weight in them to increase resistance. Games like tug-of-war and partner games like hand wrestling, Chinese get-up-and-push-me-over (partners in the same body positions try to push each other off balance) are excellent too.

Outside play using climbing towers, climbing frames, wall bars, and objects to crawl through will help to build muscle.

Try playing Row the Boat. Two children sit on the floor opposite each other; they join hands and rock back and forth, trying to go as far as they can in each direction. Encourage the children to be rhythmical, and to sing 'Row, row, row the boat . . .' with the movements. Speed can be increased by suggesting windy weather, rough seas and so on.

STRENGTHENING HAND FUNCTION

STARTING WITH SCISSORS

Using scissors requires the child to be able to use each finger in isolation, i.e. independently. Young children often use the wrong finger placement when cutting and this may restrict the amount of movement the child can make.

These activities can also be used during sand and water play to help prepare for both scissor skills and writing skills.

There are several stages to learning how to use scissors, but one of the most important actions to learn is opening and closing. To practise this, use tools such as barbecue tongs or salad servers to pick up objects of different sizes and textures, for example, cotton wool balls, foam pieces, aluminium foil balls, marshmallows, pom-poms or blocks. The bigger and softer the object to start with the easier it will be. You could time the child to see how many he can pick up in one minute, record this and encourage him to achieve a personal best.

Alternatively, make dots using a hole-punch held in one hand. Vary the thickness of the paper to increase the pressure needed to make the holes.

Use things that involve a squeezing type action – staplers and squirt guns, for example – together with items like balloons, body paints, soap and suds for games such as:

o trying to hit a suspended target (balloons) with a squirt gun
o washing body paints off each other's feet with a squirt gun
o squirting (coloured) water into a bowl of soapsuds to make bubbles
o playing blow football with a pipette or bulb squeezer
o making dot paintings using an eye-dropper and paint.

TEARING

Use this activity if the child is having difficulty placing fingers in the scissor holes. Tearing paper is a good activity to help finger isolation and if the activity is graded using thicker and thinner paper this can help strengthen the fingers as well.

Start with tissue paper and get the child to tear wide strips, gradually increasing the thickness of the paper and making the strips narrower. Move on to using old junk mail to tear up, and make collages from the different pieces of paper. You could also try using old Christmas cards and tearing strips or shapes that can then be used to make a picture. At each stage encourage the child to use his thumb and index finger.

SNIPPING

Practise snipping by cutting straws and thin strips of card or play dough. This just involves the opening and closing movement and does not require the scissors to move in a forward motion.

Then prepare strips of paper in different colours, not wider than 2 cms. Demonstrate how to snip the paper with one cut. Collect all the cuttings in a bag and you could use these for an art project.

Alternatively, get the child to snip at pieces of light-grade sandpaper. This is easier for the child to cut than paper as it is firmer to hold. He could also colour the sandpaper with crayons before cutting.

Take cotton material. Paint glue all over it and let it dry, then use it the next day. The glue makes the material stiff, so easier for children to cut. This could then be used to create a collage.

SCISSORS – TEARING AND SNIPPING

Primary school

Moving from pre-school to primary school can feel like a huge leap for the child with DCD, who may still lack many of the skills that other children take for granted.

Encourage visits with parents or guardians before the start of term and show the child where strategic places are in the school, for example, the toilets, headteacher's office and the canteen. If possible, allow the child to visit and stay for lunch – this could take place before the other children come in for their meal.

Speak to the parents about the school day so that they can talk through this with the child as well. The parents should be given the name and contact details of the special educational needs coordinator (SENCO) in case they have any concerns. If there is a school uniform it's also useful to check that the child has practised any fastenings that may be unfamiliar.

Find out if the child has any difficulties managing to eat food. Some children with DCD don't like certain textures of food or the child may still not be competent using a knife and fork.

Make other staff aware that the child may be more vulnerable at times such as breaktimes or even managing to use the toilets. The child may get more tired than other children, so teachers need to be aware that he may not 'perform' as well in the afternoon as compared with the morning.

A story board can be used in the class as a visual timetable to let the child know what is happening during the school day.

Think about all the different parts of the school day and the subject areas – ideally this should be done with the child so that he can understand the different sections and can relate better to the story board. Create a picture using drawings, computer images or where possible take photos using a digital camera. For example, the first thing the child does when he comes into school is take off and hang up his coat, so take a picture of the child's coat and peg. If the child has different books for different subjects such as numeracy, a picture of the book could be used for the story board. This again will give the child a visual prompt to see which book he needs to get. These pictures should then be placed on a sheet on the wall where the child can reach easily to take them off the story board after each activity has been completed. Laminating the pictures and placing them on a Velcro strip can make the story board more versatile.

This can be set up each day, perhaps just before home time, ready for the following day's activities.

MAKING A STORY BOARD

A TOOL KIT FOR CLASS

It is a good idea to have a writing 'tool kit' in the class so that children can try out a range of pens and pencils and grips, choosing the ones that suit them best. Allow all children to have the option of using different tools as this will reduce the possibility of the child feeling 'different'.

The tool box could be a container with a variety of equipment, including different types of rulers, pens and pencils as well as a range of pen grips. Allow the child to try and see what works best for them rather than overly directing their choices.

There is no special writing tool for the child with DCD. Different children will be helped by different pens and pencils and this will depend on the shape of their hands and the stability of their joints. Some children like a triangular pencil, others may not.

Pencil grips come in a variety of shapes and sizes and some may make the child's writing worse. Have different colours in the same type of grip, otherwise the child may choose the grip by colour preference and not the one that best suits him. Get the child to experiment with the grips and look at the results, then encourage him to choose the handwriting that looks the best. Have a large pencil sharpener that is stable and can sit on a table – a small one may be difficult to manipulate.

As well as pens and pencils, it's worth considering other writing aids for your tool kit. Some children with DCD have poor posture and can appear 'floppy'. This results in the child not being able to support his head, resting it either on his hand or on the desk when completing table-top tasks, particularly writing. An angle board can help with this, supporting the child's arm and enabling him to write more freely. It also helps the child to sit in a better position, with the added benefit of him being more able to see and hear what is going on in the classroom. Angle boards come in large and small sizes and in a number of different materials, including Perspex, plastic and wood. When choosing, think about the size and design and the flexibility of usage. Check if it fits in a drawer rather than being so big that it takes up too much desk space and makes it harder to sit the child near other children. It's a good idea to put a piece of

Dycem (non-slip matting) on the angle board to stop books moving when placed on it. Consider also using a book rest, which will place the book in a good position for copying or reading.

Seating wedges might be useful too, as they encourage the user to adopt a better posture by placing their hips in a more forward position. Always remember the child's feet should be placed firmly on the floor.

An ordered start to the day will help the child with DCD. He needs to know where to put his possessions and also what will be happening throughout the day and if there are any changes that have not been planned for, such as a replacement teacher. Constancy of the environment can have a knock-on effect on confidence.

In the cloakroom the child should have a place for his coat that is easy to see as he comes through the door. Use a photo of the child as well as his name for his coatpeg. Ask the parent to also put a name or coloured tag inside the coat so the child can easily distinguish it if it falls on the ground or gets muddled with others.

The child may need additional help putting on and taking off his coat when going out and coming in from play. What may seem an easy task for most children may be difficult and confusing for the child with DCD. He may put on the coat upside down, for example, and be unaware of his errors. Give the child a guide of how to do this task if he is encountering problems. Verbal cues such as, 'Where does the collar go?' are helpful. Teach the child an order to put it on and a method for him to check to ensure that he is doing it right. You may want to use counting such as 'collar – 1, arm – 2, front – 3' to reinforce this learning.

Try not to reorganize the classroom furniture too many times. This could totally disorientate the child and cause him to become distressed. If the layout of the room is to be altered, try to place visual prompts on the top or on the front of cupboards showing what is inside, as this will help the child when looking for things like mathematics equipment or books.

One big change from pre-school to 'big school' is going into assembly. This can be noisy and will also require the child to sit still, sometimes for a considerable length of time. The child with dyspraxia may not only find it harder to sit still but may also be uncomfortable. He may appear fidgety or look as if he is day-dreaming and not attending to what is happening. The noise made by other children may also be disturbing.

Consider allowing the child to sit either cross-legged or let him wriggle a little. Sitting the child at the end of a line of children may be easier than in the middle of a row, so that if he does fidget or move he is not disturbing or bumping into other children. If you sit the child on a low chair or supported with his back against the wall it may make the difference between him listening and taking in what is being said or concentrating instead on his discomfort. It can also be a good idea to sit him next to the same child every time in assembly as he will find this reassuring.

Remember, being in assembly for the duration may be very difficult and he may benefit from being gradually introduced to it.

WORKING IN A GROUP

Working within a group could prove more challenging for several reasons. The child may not have the social skills required to participate in a group situation. He may not be able to perform some of the required tasks at the same pace as his peers and/or he may not have understood the instructions being given. Turn-taking may also need to be explained rather than assumed.

Teaching other social rules may be necessary. The child may act socially more like a younger child and not have the ability or skills to work well in a group. He may prefer to watch rather than fully participate.

Some children need to face the board and the teacher to take in all the information. Having to turn around to look at the whiteboard and listen may be hard to do, so try positioning the child near to the teacher or a classroom assistant who can check understanding and repeat instructions. Having a buddy for group tasks can also help, as different skills can be harnessed and the difficulties made less obvious.

Let the child know you are coming to him next in a group task. Pre-arrange a signal such as walking past and tapping him on his shoulder or patting your hand on the desk. The child can then be prepared. If you are uncertain about touching the child, perhaps this could be discussed with the parent and the child and you can agree together what the sign will be.

When you are allocating jobs to individuals in the group, base your choices on areas of strength rather than weakness. For example, if the group is working on a science project and the child has difficulty recording work but is good at solving problems, this could be his role in the group.

Always check that the child understands what is expected of him. He will have to work harder to concentrate on the interactions and may get more tired than the others in his group. Allow him a break if this is the case.

Any techniques introduced early to teach organizational skills for the child with DCD will be helpful. These include organizing himself as well as organizing his work on paper.

Make techniques clear and usable to the individual – discuss the techniques/strategies with the child and get him to think about ideas to help himself. He will need to understand the reason why he is using the technique and how it will help him; for example, using a timer will allow him to complete his tasks on time and not be later than others.

When working with a younger child, place his work in a tray or on a desk and have his name or a photo clearly visible so that he can find it easily. Try using the same coloured tray and folders so that they correspond and the child associates his possessions, and a place for them, with the same colour. This will speed up accessing equipment and tidying up at the end of the class.

Use a clear pencil case with the contents labelled inside so that the child can see his possessions and encourage him to put them back in at the end of class.

Start using a 'to do' list, even with quite young children. To begin with it need only have about three items on it. If the child cannot read, it could be made using visual symbols. This will help the child to break tasks into small steps and see the goal he is working towards.

If the child has difficulty knowing where to start and finish on the page, place a green spot where he should start writing and a red spot for where he needs to stop.

GAINING ORGANIZATIONAL SKILLS

NEGATIVE BEHAVIOUR

Change makes us all anxious, but for the dyspraxic child not knowing what to do and where to go may make him more withdrawn or 'act out' his frustrations on himself or others. An example of this could be if the child is playing a game with other children but not understanding the rules fully. He gets them wrong, misinterpreting what he should be doing, and then gets told off by his peers for being silly.

If the child exhibits sudden negative behaviour such as hitting out, check what has happened before the event. This may be a demonstration of a lack of understanding or increased anxiety due to being unsure of what was going to happen next.

Look to see if there is a pattern to the behaviour of the child – this will allow you to pre-empt any negative behaviour before it starts. Be clear with the child that you understand the reason why he behaved in a certain way, but not his response. Encourage him to talk through why something happened.

Suggest to parents that they create a timetable at home and mark on it key activities in the week, so that the child can then develop a sense of 'shape' to the week and knows, for example, that PE is on a Wednesday and Friday. You can also help to prepare the child for any changes by talking to him about alterations in staff or the curriculum.

Some children will find adapting to any change in their routine difficult. Within the class these children will present themselves as anxious, and they need reassuring.

Give the child plenty of notice if their routine is to be changed. Small changes to you can be big for the child – for example, if the child is to have a packed lunch when he is used to a cooked lunch in school or he is going on a school trip.

If you are going somewhere outside the school, ensure that the child knows where the toilets are, and if bottom-wiping is a problem suggest parents provide wet wipes. If you are planning on having food out, explain where he will eat it and when.

It's helpful to make a laminated card which has stick-on Velcro squares showing a list of all the activities taking place. Then, if any last minute changes are made, have some empty laminated squares and write on these so they can be used quickly.

COPING WITH CHANGE

MAINTAINING SELF-ESTEEM

Self-esteem among children with DCD has been shown to be lower when compared to other children.

It is important to recognize the efforts that the child may have made in school and try and seek opportunities for him to win an award or recognition so that others can see his success. Establish an award that will show others the child's areas of strength and allow him to gain self-esteem. It might be the opportunity to go on an outing or being the one to choose a film to watch in school with others. A points scheme is one way for the child to work towards the award – seeing points accumulating can be motivating. Points should be awarded for effort and not for output, as the child with DCD will have to work harder than his peers to achieve similar or less output.

It's also a good idea to give the child some responsibility within the class so that others can see his skills. This privilege should be earned, again by effort, so that other children do not think that he is being favoured. Praise positive behaviour and try and ignore any negative statements the child may make.

Consider introducing non-team-based sports so the child can join in, such as swimming, rambling, badminton, trampolining or even yoga.

The child with DCD often has poor concepts of time. He will not understand the idea that something needs to be completed in five minutes; for example, the class is told that they need to have their books put away in five minutes and the child with DCD is seen still carrying on working, seemingly unaware that he needs to pack up and prepare for the end of the lesson.

Externalize time for the child – he needs to see, hear or feel time as a reminder since his 'inner body clock' may not be telling him that it is time to move on to another task.

Use a timer, such as an egg timer, a digital or analogue clock or kitchen timer, so that the child can be alerted when time has passed and he has to move on to another task. Do not expect him to learn this readily as he may always need to continue to use external reminders like watches and alarms to remind him that tasks need to be completed.

Give the child clear goals to work on. Many children with DCD have difficulties being able to visualize the end goal. It may appear unclear and distant to him. Work with the child to learn to set goals and provide him with a framework to do this, such as techniques for him to get his ideas down onto paper.

TEACHING TIME CONCEPTS

IDEA

27

Children with DCD find a non-structured environment such as the playground at breaktime more difficult to deal with than the structured environment of a classroom. The child may get more tired and need time out to recover. The noise in the playground may be harder to cope with and at times having a quiet place to sit may be helpful. Any provisions set up for the child should be disseminated to all staff to ensure consistency.

Make sure there is a buddy system or create a 'talking post' in the playground where children can meet and talk if they want to. Try to encourage friendship groups such as using a 'circle of friends' if some children are being isolated from their peer group.

Children with DCD are more likely to be bullied and breaktimes are times when this may occur. During a PSHE lesson define and discuss the 'problem' (don't make the child the problem). To evoke empathy and affirm their role in helping to move things forward, ask the group how they would feel if they were left out and how they can make all children feel involved at play time. You can teach the child with DCD to be assertive by relaxing his body (deep breathing helps), keeping his hands steady and using frequent eye contact. These tricks help children seem self-assured, even when they are not.

Encourage problem solving, even at a young age, if there are disputes in the playground. This is especially important for the child with DCD, who may need these skills in many aspects of his life.

Providing skipping ropes and balls for the children to use in the playground can also help, as activities can be semi-structured.

Most children with DCD will find games such as football or any group ball game harder to play and so may be seen to be watching from the edges rather than joining in. It may be worth considering a range of alternative games that help motor skills and can be done in smaller groups or in twos and threes. It is useful also if the child with DCD can be a part of the choosing of the games, rather than being the last to participate. If playing a game of tag, start some of the time with the child with DCD being 'it'.

Try playing games like French skipping. This requires a long piece of elastic. Two people stand one at each end with the elastic stretched between them at ankle height. and then one person jumps in while songs are chanted. There are a number of songs that can be used and this activity can be undertaken with either one or two children jumping in between the elastic. If the child has considerable difficulty taking part he can stand at one end of the elastic and join in some of the chants, learning this part first.

You could also mark the playground to play hopscotch, which is a useful game for improving both fine and gross motor skills. Other simple games using skill-building equipment such as hula hoops and quoits could be introduced.

Lots of children like to play Jacks, but try using a larger bouncy ball rather than a small rubber ball. A larger ball will be easier to catch, or alternatively use a foam ball which may be a little slower.

Red Letter is nice game to play as it doesn't require good motor skills. A person is picked to be the leader. He stands with his back to the rest of the players who stand ten metres away from him. The leader calls a letter of the alphabet (for example 'a'). If a player's name contains that letter, the player can move a step forward. The number of steps forward depends on the number of times that letter in his name occurs. The leader continues calling out letters until someone reaches them.

Lunchtime can be difficult for a number of reasons. It can start from the moment of not knowing who to sit next to. Often children with DCD have fewer friends and may not have someone particular to sit with. Arrange the seating positions for all children so that the choices are taken away from the pupils themselves; everyone has a chance of sitting next to a different child and greater opportunities for mixing are created.

Some children with DCD may not like certain textures of food and will avoid eating them altogether. If made to eat these foods they may even be physically sick. Find out from parents what difficulties the child may have around food and mealtimes and let the lunchtime supervisors know.

The child with DCD may find using a knife and fork harder to do efficiently and may spill and drop food or avoid using cutlery altogether, using his fingers in preference. Opening a lunchbox, drinking flask or bottle may also be difficult if the clip on it is too tight or there is a straw to insert. Work in class on bilateral activities (using both hands working together) that will improve skills for successful lunchtimes. Use mock sausages made from play dough, and special knives and forks; practise in class cutting sausages into slices (this could be incorporated in the numeracy lesson for adding, subtracting or fractions). Handwriting activities will also help with eating skills as they involve bilateral work. If necessary, consider obtaining some specialist cutlery or bend a set of cheap cutlery so that the angle of the spoon or fork is tilted to aid usage. Check that the child is sitting appropriately.

Some schools have a queuing system where children have to carry their food and a drink on a tray and need to balance this and negotiate space at the same time. This may result in spills and falls. Try placing some non-slip matting such as Dycem under the plate or use a dampened tea towel. If the child tends to spill food down his front, before he starts to eat suggest he removes his top layer of clothing, such as a jumper. Then if he does spill anything it will be hidden by the jumper when it is put back on. Alternatively, a change of clothes could be kept for the child in a place where he can change without others necessarily knowing.

Making sure the child is placed in a position where he can listen to the teacher and see what is going on is important. If he has to turn around all the time he will have to regain his stability and may lose concentration as a consequence; also he may cause others around him to become distracted.

Place the child so that he faces the teacher and he does not need to move to listen to instructions being given. Who the child sits next to may be important. This is often like a jigsaw puzzle in a class of 30, and may be difficult to get right. The child with DCD may not always be spatially aware and may be likely to take up more space on the desk or move into someone else's area without realizing he is doing so. If he is left-handed, try to find another left-handed child or place him on the left-hand side of the desk.

The child may need to have his 'space' marked out on the table – use coloured tape for this – so he can see his boundaries and stay within them. You could do the same for the other children so as not to highlight the child as different.

Allow the child movement breaks, as he may find it difficult to stay still for any length of time and his fidgeting may interrupt the other children. Give him a 'chore' to do, such as collecting up books or giving out books or pens, so that it is not obvious that he is being allowed to move around.

THE CLASSROOM SEATING PLAN

IDEA 31

IMPROVING LETTER FORMATION

It is important to develop a good concept of letter shapes. There are a number of fun activities you can use to help with this. Try some of these ideas, using letters on a grand scale.

Put children in pairs and get one child to paint water on the playground in letter shapes and the other partner to guess the letter. Use a large paint brush or small roller and a bucket or put the water into a paint tray and use this to paint letters. They could also spell out 'secret' messages to one another. Writing on the playground using large chunky chalks is an alternative idea. Encourage the child to make large letters to reinforce the shapes.

Indoors, try getting a sand tray and using the end of a paintbrush to 'write' large letter shapes. The increased physical pressure needed helps the child to reinforce the shapes. Alternatively, fill a paint tray with shaving foam and get the children to write with their fingers in this. Creating letter shapes in the air using scarves or ribbons on sticks can also be fun.

Try attaching a large piece of drawing paper to the wall. Make an outline or shape across the page, and then down the page. Using a marker pen, have the child trace over your line from left to right, or from top to bottom. Trace each figure at least ten times, then have the child draw the figure next to your model several times.

You could develop this by playing connect the dots. Again make sure the child's strokes connect dots in the right direction from left to right, and from top to bottom. You can place a green dot on the left-hand side to remind him where to start.

If you haven't got the space to try some of the larger activities suggested in Idea 31, there are plenty of other ways to develop letter formation.

Cut out letters from sandpaper and let the child feel the shape of the letters. Try using raised lined paper so the child can see where to place the letters on the line.

You could also create templates of writing patterns and get the child first to go over the shapes and then to copy them – use zigzags, snakes, etc. The templates could be laminated and a semi-permanent pen used, which wipes off allowing repeat use.

Most children love using stencils. Get them to trace around the stencil – the non-dominant hand should hold the stencil flat and stable against the paper, while the dominant hand pushes the pencil firmly against the edge of the stencil. The stencil must be held firmly. Use a small piece of Dycem or Blu-Tak stuck under a plastic stencil to help it stay in place.

Use a Magna Doodle or a similar toy that allows writing to be wiped away or a wipe-on/wipe-off board. Try practising vertical, horizontal and parallel lines.

BETTER LETTER FORMATION – TABLE-TOP IDEAS

Choosing the right pencil or pen is important to aid the child's writing. Pencil grips are often used with children with DCD. There is not one grip or pen that is right for all children.

If the child has a very tight grip, you may want to try to put a pencil through a plastic golf ball and get the child to hold the golf ball; this can get his hand in a better position. A cheap way of making a pencil grip is to use several elastic bands on the pencil or to get a small piece of foam tubing and put this on the pencil.

The size is important too. Chunky pencils may be easier to handle than very thin ones, and a shorter pencil is easier to use than a long one. If you only have long pencils, try snapping one in half.

If sharpening a pencil is difficult, then consider using a retractable pencil. These are also good for grading the amount of pressure the child uses when writing – if the lead breaks the child will need to lighten his grip.

Attach a pen or pencil to a lanyard or plastic wrist coil that can be attached to trousers, so pens don't get lost or misplaced as easily.

The way the child grasps a pencil may not always be the traditional grip. Check to see whether he seems to be gripping his pen too tightly – you may see the fingers whiten or his forefinger bending or hyper-extended rather than remaining extended. Look and see if the index finger is red and the knuckle white from too much pressure.

If the child chooses an alternative grip, don't change it if it is working for him. He may be changing the grip to create a position of stability. Try getting the child to pretend to grip tightly a small stone in his fingers and count to ten. Discuss how his hand feels. Next, get him to pretend to gently hold a feather in his fingertips, and count to ten. Discuss how his hand now feels. Help him to understand he can write faster and for a longer time when his hand is more relaxed.

Games to help improve grasp such as Pick-up Sticks, threading beads and peg games are useful.

FINGER POSITION – GETTING A GRIP

STARTING ON CONCEPT MAPPING

In preparation for secondary school some children may find concept mapping a useful technique to learn as it is a good way to organize thoughts and start to put ideas into writing.

There are two ways of doing concept mapping, either on paper or using a computer version. Start first with a paper-based one to teach the child the technique. A simple way to get ideas onto paper initially may be to use Post-it® notes. Get the child to put down ideas on the paper and stick them on a wall, then move them around into groups.

Introduce the idea of concept mapping by getting the child to come up with suggestions about a topic they want to write about. Ask him if he can see pictures in his *mind* when he talks about each word, and show examples so he can see how words and pictures are often linked together and help us plan stories. Write some of the words down on the whiteboard and show how you could group them together and then find link words to label each group. Demonstrate how this could be turned into a concept map and words could be substituted with pictures or pictures added in to aid memory. Adding in colour will show how this can reinforce different areas of the concept map. Get the child to try this himself and then practise this skill by reading a short passage and asking the child to make a concept map, outlining the important information in the passage.

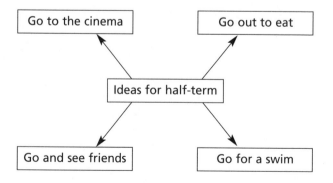

The pre-school section highlights a number of activities to help children gain scissor skills and these can be developed with the primary school child.

Get the child to line up the top blade of the scissors with the line to be cut. He can practise this by cutting short pieces of paper or straws as this focuses on the line to cut rather than on moving the scissors forward. He should cut slowly using small cuts. The blades of the scissors should not be closed fully (you can pretend that the blades are the jaws of a crocodile which do not close completely). When attempting to cut curved lines the scissors and the paper should both be turned.

Encourage cutting with both 'thumbs up' – hold the paper with the thumb on top and hold the scissors with the thumb above the other fingers. Sometimes children are not sure which way to place their thumbs in the scissors and place them down. Draw two eyes and a mouth on their thumbs and tell them to cut with the 'face' looking at them.

The website www.dltk-kids.com/crafts/miscellaneous/ scissor_skills.htm has a number of activity sheets that can be printed out for the child to practise cutting out different shapes.

USING SCISSORS CORRECTLY

Try practising cutting in one direction using the suggestions below. Initially use thicker paper as it is often easier to control.

○ Punch a hole or cluster of holes at the top and bottom of a sheet of paper. Get the child to cut from one hole towards the direction of the other holes.

○ Randomly glue coloured stickers on card or paper. Tell the child to cut from spot to spot. The larger the stickers the better the chance of success.

○ Make two templates using thick cardboard or wood. Sandwich some paper between the templates and get the child to cut the paper using the templates to help guide the scissors.

○ Glue two lollipop sticks parallel to each other on a sheet of stiff paper. Cut the paper between the sticks. Repeat, gradually bringing the sticks closer together.

○ Glue two pieces of wool parallel to each other. Cut between the wool strips. Gradually glue wool strips closer together.

○ Glue a number of coloured strips across the paper approximately 2 cms in width. Cut within the coloured areas.

Also try these activities to help cut along a line:

○ Cut strips of thin card, then glue the strips into circles to make paper chains.

○ Punch a line of holes along the edge of a piece of paper then cut along the strip.

○ Draw a line near to the edge of the paper. Cut strips up to the line. Fold alternate flaps up and cut along them.

There is now a vast range of adapted scissors available for children who are having difficulty using conventional types.

For children who are unable to master the opening and closing action, try using training scissors. These have two sets of finger holes, one for the child and one for you. This will give the child the opportunity to experience the feel of the movement needed to use the scissors.

For children who don't appear to have the strength to open and close the scissors, try 'long loop' scissors. These allow the child to place all fingers in the hole, enabling him to use all his strength. They are also sprung, so are easier to open and close.

There are a variety of other scissors available – make up a box with a range and let the child try them himself so he can see which best suits him and is most comfortable to use. See www.peta-uk.com for a good range of different types of scissors.

IDEA

38

CHOOSING SCISSORS

IDEA 39

Number work, such as learning times tables, is often hard for the child with DCD to grasp. It is important first to ensure the child understands number concepts, and making numbers 'real' will help.

Kits such as Numicon (www.numicon.co.uk) are great for this. Numicon is a mathematics programme that can be used from a young age and has different size and colour shapes with holes in them to represent the different numbers. It also has 'pegs' which can be placed on a board to aid number correspondence concepts. The children can see and feel the numbers – and logically, the bigger the number the larger the shape.

Try making number shapes out of plasticine or play dough and relate this also to objects when counting. This will help the child to see and feel the shapes and build up number concepts.

Understanding the 'language' of mathematics will also help. For example, the child with DCD needs to know that '+, add, plus, and, addition' all mean the same thing.

Play games such as snakes and ladders, darts, dominoes and others that depend on numbers, counting, calculation and scoring, as they are great for making mathematics easier to understand.

The more 'real' the examples of mathematics are, the easier it will be for the child to grasp the concepts. Cookery can be a useful way to learn weights and measures, fractions and ratios. An old-fashioned set of balance scales is ideal. Count out spoonfuls of ingredients.

Using calendars and timelines in history can also help with mathematics.

Learning times tables is usually undertaken through the 'auditory' route of reciting and repeating the tables. This may not be the best route for some children with DCD, as their auditory memory may be not as strong as other methods of learning. Repeating the tables again and again may not embed the tables fully and result in the child becoming increasingly frustrated.

Different techniques, such as seeing the numbers build up, may be better. This can be done by using kits such as Numicon (see Idea 39), where the child can feel the numbers increase and there is a logical and visual pattern to them. Computer programs such as *Numbershark* help improve numeracy skills and understanding. *Numbershark* features several different games covering addition, subtraction, multiplication and division in ways which add meaning and understanding to these operations.

There are several good websites with plenty of tips for teaching and learning times tables. Have a look at:

○ www.teachingtables.co.uk/
○ www.multiplication.com/teach.htm/

PE AND GAMES – ADAPTING SESSIONS

Physical education can be a challenge for children with DCD, but also an opportunity to improve fine and gross motor skills, as well as balance and coordination. Improved confidence and self-esteem here can tip into the classroom as a consequence. Check what the developmental level of the child is; for example, it is no good doing ball games requiring dodging and avoiding if the child cannot run in a straight line. Grading the games for success is also essential, as the child needs to be motivated and see that the end goal is attainable.

Changing from school clothes to PE clothes may be a challenge for many young children with DCD who may not have acquired these basic independent living skills. It's a good idea to let parents know what day the child has PE so he can wear clothes which are easier to take off and put on. Remind parents that shoes with Velcro rather than laces are much easier to change. You could provide each child with a box for his clothes, so at least socks and other articles of clothing don't get mixed up.

Some children will find orientating their clothing difficult – knowing which way their shirt, skirt or trousers go on may be hard and may require extra assistance. Encourage the child to recognize tags on the back of a T-shirt, for example, or a school logo on the front, as a guide to orientation. It also helps if when changing shoes or clothes the child is stable. A chair to sit on will make dressing and undressing tasks much easier, especially taking shoes and socks on and off, as long as the chair is not too big and the child's legs are not dangling down. Alternatively, allow him to sit on the floor and lean against a wall.

The child may need additional time for dressing. However, if he is always the last to get to PE he may also miss the first instructions being given. Try to get the child to the class at the same time as the others if possible or make sure that initial instructions are repeated.

At the end of a school day most children with DCD will be more tired than their peers. They will have had to work harder to complete the same volume of work. Facing the task of doing any homework may be too much and can result in a battle between the parent and the child.

Try to reduce the volume of written work taken home and have homework instructions written down for him, perhaps on stickers that could be stuck into a diary. Worksheets that require single-word answers are a good way of reducing the amount of writing to be done. Alternatively, you could allow the parent to scribe for the child (the parent can initial the work they have recorded).

If you can, let the child use a tape recorder for composing stories, rather than writing them. This allows him the freedom to be creative. Often children with DCD will write short – rather than long – stories because of the effort writing causes them, but they may be verbally much more able.

Children with DCD may not have as wide a circle of friends as their peers and may not have others to call on if they have misunderstood homework or have not been able to get it all written down. Pair up parents as homework 'buddies' so they know who to call if there are queries over homework.

A homework diary recorded by an adult (such as a teaching assistant) is helpful, as the child may be focusing on what to do next at the end of the lesson and may not be able to listen and record instructions at the same time.

GIVING HOMEWORK

**IDEA**

43

PREPARING FOR THE NEXT DAY

A tired child will not work effectively when he arrives at school. He will also be anxious if he is worrying about forgetting various items he may need such as sports kit. Work with the parents to ensure the child is prepared for the following day.

Suggest that bags are packed the night before and placed by the front door and clothes are laid out on the floor in the order they will be put on. Recommend that the child has a timetable on the wall in his bedroom so he knows which classes he will be doing the following day. Parents can be encouraged to work on time management skills, using timers for tasks at home such as showering or homework to reinforce these skills.

Ask parents to let you know how long homework is taking and limit the length of time the child should spend on the work.

Prepare the child in advance for the trip. Talk through what will happen and, if it is part of a project, explain why you are going and what information he needs to be looking for while on the trip. Check that the note that was sent home has arrived at the parents' home and is not still in the bottom of a school bag!

The child with DCD should have someone to sit with on the coach and not be the last to be seated. Ideally he should be told the day before who he is sitting with to prevent him becoming anxious overnight.

School trips often involve note-taking or filling in worksheets. If there is writing to be done, pair the child with a partner who does not mind doing this. If the child has to stand or walk and write at the same time it could cause him more difficulties. It's useful to have a buddy system for all the children so that the young person does not get lost in a new environment, but does not feel different from others.

When you send the initial note home about the trip, remember to remind parents to supply food that is easy to open and to use disposable containers so that there are fewer things to lose. Encourage all children to have clothes labelled.

SCHOOL TRIPS

IDEA 45

SWIMMING

Most primary schools at some point will take children swimming. The child with DCD may find changing and organizing his clothes difficult. He may also have the following difficulties: dressing while wet, difficulty balancing to put on shoes and not being able to plan sufficiently to place clothes in an order or to hang them up. He is likely to need more time than his peers to get dressed, and may become anxious if he feels pressured and needs to rush to be ready to get back on the bus for school. Rushing may make the child more 'clumsy' than normal and this in turn could cause him to drop his clothes which may then become wet, or he may slip and fall.

Make sure you give the child a basket where he can place his clothes to keep them together and that he wears clothes on swimming days that are easy to get on and off. Keeping a spare set of clothes in school is a good plan. You will need to allow extra time when changing.

When entering the pool, encourage the child to put both hands on the side of the pool and turn over onto his front to slide in so he can stay in control. He will be better using the steps to get out of the pool, as pulling himself up on the side may be difficult. Allow plenty of space for the child to move so that he doesn't hit or kick the other children around him.

Specific activities can be done in the water to help the child with DCD. For example, marching on the spot and then walking forward and backwards through the water will help strengthen the legs. Other exercises, such as holding onto the side of the pool, lying on the tummy and kicking the legs, climbing in and out of the water, throwing a soft ball with other children, will be helpful. Some children will find coordinating arms and legs difficult, so consider allowing them to use flippers as this will help them to move through the water and give them confidence. You could also introduce a float – the child rests it under his arms or chest and just moves his legs.

Clubs and after-school activities may be supervised by volunteer parents or teachers other than the class teachers. These people will not know the child so well and should be given information and guidance on how to grade any activity to ensure that the child can participate alongside his peers. It may also be necessary first to check what level of skill the child has and not to assume he has prior knowledge of the game or activity and its rules.

If the club is at the end of the day the child may be tired and not have the stamina to keep up with his peers. This could cause him to appear badly behaved or less interested in the activity than his peers.

Look at the activity the children are going to do and consider some alternative ways of delivering it. If it is a ball game, use different, lighter balls that travel more slowly. If playing a game like badminton, you could use a larger shuttlecock. Explain the rules and demonstrate the game – do not rely on just telling the child what is going on as he may not be able to remember a long list of instructions. If the activity is sport related, think of ways of grading the activity to make it easier for the child.

Make sure that you speak to the teacher or leader that is taking the group and let them know of any adapted equipment the child uses in class that has helped him, such as special scissors, pencil grips, rulers or an angle board.

Ideally the activities shouldn't go on for too long and where possible should be broken up into smaller sections. Check the child's understanding of each section and allow him to gain the skills required before moving on. Be aware that learning any new skill is likely to be achieved but may take him longer than his peers.

Praise success and talk through with the child what has worked and why he thinks it has worked. He can then take the skills learnt in clubs and apply them in class.

Sports day can be a nightmare for children with coordination difficulties. The egg and spoon race, the dressing-up race and the three-legged race may exemplify where the child's skills are at their weakest. Coming last every time in every race can be soul destroying and can lead to weeks of dread before the event itself.

Encourage the child to be a helper or organizer if they don't want to participate. Could the child be the official time recorder, hold the tape at the end line or wave the flag to start the race?

Use a scheme where each child in training sessions records their times for each event before the sports day. The child with DCD can then try out the different races and decide himself which one he thinks he could improve the most and achieve a personal best in. On the day the challenge is to beat his personal time. This allows the child to participate alongside his peers, but also to compete and be a winner. Each child can then be awarded gold, silver or bronze based on their efforts on the day. Take time to observe the child during PE lessons and look at his areas of strength.

Could you consider an alternative sports day?

The school could create a fête and have stalls as well as races. These could include cake and plant stalls, a raffle and game stalls such as 'soak the teacher'. You could get the children to come up with a theme such as a Victorian day, where you play games and races that were played at that time like hopscotch, skipping and cup and ball.

Games could also be organized into 'houses' and each person works at getting points for their house. Other non-sporting activities, such as cake-making, photography, art and music, or even tasks where children help out around school, could be counted towards house points.

Another idea could be to have a quiz day or a treasure hunt around school where everyone has to 'break the code' to find the treasure. This could test skills in a number of areas, with participants having to work out riddles and clues or build a raft to cross the 'water'. It will also encourage a team spirit.

These approaches allow the children to see that in any team there need to be people with different strengths, and children can therefore be taught to value these differences.

ALTERNATIVE SPORTS DAYS

IDEA

49

To teach ball skills it is useful to set up a kit which contains a variety of sizes, weights and textures of balls.

The weight of the ball will make a difference to the ease or difficulty the child has in catching it. The lighter the ball, the slower the trajectory it forms. This gives the child a greater chance to catch it successfully. Paper balls can be inflated and will move through the air very slowly, and balloons are also light and will also move slowly. Putting a bell inside the balloon before inflating it will give added sound to reinforce the direction from which the balloon is coming.

The size of the ball will also help the child with catching. A larger ball will be easier to catch and track than a smaller one. A ball with a greater surface area is also easier to play with, so try using a large foam ball. 'Pom-pom' wool balls made from two pieces of card with wool wrapped around them (making these is also a great fine motor activity) are easier to catch, or you could use a 'Koosh' ball – a rubber ball with lots of rubber threads coming from it.

Other items worth including are cones for the children to 'dribble' around and a target for the children to throw things at. The target could be made by the children or could be a cross marked on a wall or large paper circle. Bean bags can be useful for throwing practice – use a wastepaper basket, laundry basket or cardboard box for the children to throw into.

Kikaflik is one toy that has been developed to gain skills in catching. It is played using a specially designed brightly coloured board and different sized foam balls (see www.kikaflik.co.uk). It requires good timing and improves coordination skills using hands, eyes and feet.

Games to improve balance are important as they impact on other sports such as football, netball and even skipping. The child needs to be able to stand on one leg and be stable before being able to run and kick a ball.

Start off by getting the child to walk along a line forwards and backwards without stepping off. Then proceed to walking along a low beam holding a partner's or adult's hand for additional support. Alternatively, the child could use sticks held in each hand to gain stability.

Another idea is to get the children to lay out a course using stepping stones or rubber mats so they have to jump from mat to mat without falling in the 'water'. Make the distances close together to start with and then gradually move the mats further apart.

You can also use big foot stilts which look like upturned cups with ropes to hold onto. The child has to walk on these and use the ropes for support.

Trampolining will help with balance and coordination and, in addition, improve core stability. 'Maze balance boards' can be great to use as well. The child has to stand on a wobble board with a maze in it and move a small ball around the board while balancing. This can also aid attention and concentration.

Balance and coordination can be improved by working with other parts of the body, not just the legs. Try using a scooter board and place the child on his front so that he has his legs and arms off the ground. Encourage him to maintain this position and just use his arms to move. Races can also be done in pairs, going from one end of the sports hall to the other.

GAMES TO HELP BALANCE

IMPROVING SHOULDER STABILITY

Children with DCD often seem a bit 'wobbly' and find it difficult stabilizing and fixing one joint to be able to use another part of the body, for example, using hands independently of elbows and shoulders.

To help with this, play the hedgehog game. Tell the child to curl up into a tight ball with his hands around his knees. Instruct him also to touch his nose on his knees. Count how long he can hold that position. Practise with the child so he can build up the time he can maintain this.

The Bridge is another simple game you can play. Get the child to lie on his back and lift his bottom off the floor to create a bridge. Watch that the child does not push up too far or press his head too much into the mat. Check whether you can pass a toy car or other object under the bridge. Count with the child to hold the position for five seconds and then gradually build up the time to ten seconds.

Team games such as beanbag racing can be good fun too. The children have to go on all fours, crawling while carrying a beanbag on their back from one end of the room to another and depositing the beanbag in a basket. This could be done as a relay race. On the same theme you could create an obstacle course where the child needs to navigate his way through and over different objects – under a blanket, under a table and over some cushions or mats, for example.

Activities based on working in a prone position (on the stomach) on the floor will strengthen the child's back and neck and also help improve shoulder stability.

Start with racing games from one end of the hall in relays, crawling commando style, keeping the stomach as far down on the floor as possible. Another game that can be played is with a straw and a ping-pong ball. Divide the class into two teams. Each child has to blow the ping-pong ball from one end of a starting line to the finishing line while moving along on all fours.

Alternatively, get the children to pretend they have a crown on their back and they have to move along a path making sure it does not fall off, also crawling on all fours.

It can also be fun to ask the children to pretend to be different animals travelling across the floor – for example, they could be snakes, crabs or lizards. The class could play a guessing game or be given cards to pretend to be different animals.

In order to play team games such as netball, football or rugby children need to be able to negotiate other moving children around them, while they are moving as well. For the child with DCD, running and dodging together can be very hard to do.

Start off by playing a stop/start walking game. Everyone starts to walk and stops as soon as they hear the word 'stop' called. Add additional commands such as 'stop, turn right', and gradually speed up the instructions. Next, get the children to dodge one another. They must run around the playground and have to avoid running into one another. If they touch anyone they are out of the game.

You could also get the children to run around cones laid out in a line so they have to learn to change direction. Get them to run backwards around the cones and to run in different directions in response to commands.

Dodge ball is a good game for practising these skills. One child throws the ball at the others (below the knee) and if a child is hit they are then out. Using a foam ball means that there is little risk of anyone being hurt or falling over, but you could also play with a soft football. There are lots of fun variations to this game listed on the website at www.funandgames.org/dodgeball.htm/

Ball skills are often hard for the child with DCD to acquire. Grading the activity and allowing the child to be aware of improvement in his skills is important to maintain motivation. Encourage self-scoring so that the child can see how he has improved.

Put children into pairs and get them to sit on the floor with their legs open and to roll a large foam ball to one another. If the child is not stable in this position he could lean against a wall. Once this has been achieved get the children to catch and throw the ball in a stationary, standing position. If this is too difficult then use a ball that can bounce and add in a bounce-then-catch into the sequence to give additional time. Alternatively, a beanbag or screwed up newspaper formed into paper balls could be used. The child can try to catch and throw in different positions, such as kneeling or standing.

Next get the child to throw a beanbag/balloon/scarf in the air and catch it. Once this has been achieved the child can add a clap into the routine before catching it.

Once some basic throwing and catching skills have been acquired, it can be fun to create targets for the children to aim at – empty water or fizzy drink bottles filled with sand are ideal for this.

Encourage the child to talk through his errors and how he thinks he could improve his performance next time. A guided approach is useful and allows him to internalize what he is doing and how he can make a difference. He may find copying others harder and may need to feel the action himself. Allow him to talk through his movements as he is making them.

CATCHING AND THROWING GAMES

KICKING ACTIVITIES

Before a child can kick a ball he must be able to stand on one leg, but balance can be a problem. First try blowing bubbles and get the child to stamp out the bubbles. You could also blow up balloons and see if the child can burst the balloon.

Next, place children in pairs and get them to kick a ball back and forth to one another. Make sure they are standing quite close to one another so they can successfully kick it, stop it and then kick it back. Once they can do this, get each pair to move further back from one another and repeat the activity, then gradually move further and further away from one another.

Let the child with DCD practise kicking a ball into a large goal. Encourage the child to stand close to the goal to start with, and slowly move back as he has success. Start from a standing position and then move to a running kick.

Another exercise is to get the child to put the ball on the ground and walk along keeping the ball close to his feet. He must then stop the ball by putting his foot on top of it. Reinforce the idea that the child needs to watch the ball.

Number concepts can be harder for children with DCD to grasp, and seeing and touching the numbers can help a great deal. Introducing numbers in a fun way and improving gross motor skills at the same time can be a great combination.

Try making a fishing game. Take some sticks (these could be bamboo canes used for the garden) and place hooks into the ends of each one. Secure some string with a magnet on the end of these. Make some 'fish' numbers and attach a paper clip to the edge of each one (you could do this in class, practising cutting activities with scissors). Ask the children to 'fish' for specific numbers. Each fish could also have spots on it as well as the number, to reinforce numeric concepts. Develop the game by asking the children to find combinations like 'two numbers that add up to seven'. If you change the position for fishing (kneeling, sitting, standing), the child is also working on different sets of muscles.

Another idea is to get the child to count balls while catching and throwing. Try also practising times tables by getting the child to count in twos, for example, each time he catches the ball.

A good way of introducing the concepts of division and multiplication is to place hoops out on the floor of the sports hall. Ask the children to divide into groups of threes or fours and stand inside the hoops. There may be children left out. Get them to add up how many children are in the hoops and how many are left out.

Working on batting skills can also help with numeracy. The children have to hit screwed up paper balls into a laundry basket set a few feet away and count how many times they can do it successfully. They can record this in a table and compare and contrast scores.

PE AND NUMBER WORK

IDEA 57

Exercises that can strengthen hand function will assist the child in improving fine motor skills. Here are some simple things for you to try.

○ Squeezy toys – use a washing up liquid bottle, fill it with paint and squeeze out the paint to make pictures. Use different bottles for different colours.

○ Oven baster – use this to get the child to suck up water or paint and to squeeze it out on to the paper, making different shapes.

○ Peg games – use a variety of different size pegs, from large quilt pegs to tiny pegs, for activities such as clipping them to the side of an ice cream carton. This could be turned into a game and played in pairs. Each child starts with the same number of pegs and has to throw a dice and clip on the number of pegs he throws. The first one to clip all their pegs on the container wins. Alternatively, all pegs could be clipped to the container and the child has to remove the number that he throws.

○ Scrunching paper – use tissue paper and get the child first to tear it into strips and then to scrunch it up into balls. This could be used for making a collage.

○ Wrap an elastic band around the thumb and index finger and slowly stretch open and slowly close. Grade the activity with the thickness of the elastic band, or the number of times it is wrapped around.

○ Working with play dough – this is an ideal medium for hand-strengthening exercises. Get the child to make balls and roll them out with his hands. Start with thick rolls and then get the child to roll them out to thinner snakes. He can also make different sized balls, working both hands together.

You need good visual perception and visual memory in order to copy from a board – remembering what you have seen and being able to translate it onto paper.

Using form boards or magnetic letters, play a recognition game. Starting with a limited number of letters, ask the child to recognize a letter and then place it in order of the alphabet (for younger children, use the 'ABC' song). Place several letters face up on the table and ask the child to find a specific letter. Try using stickers that are letters for this game, then the child can peel the letter off.

Alternatively, place an alphabet strip before the child. Draw part of a letter such as a circle. Ask the child to find and draw as many letters as he can that include this shape.

Kim's Game can be excellent for improving memory. It is a development of the simple memory games suggested in the Pre-school section. Place up to 24 articles of different kinds – for example, a key, a pocket knife, a computer disk, a coin, a marble, a comb – on a table and cover with a cloth. The child steps up to the table, and the cloth is removed for exactly one minute; the child then looks, trying to remember as many items as possible. Once the cloth is put back on he has to write down the items he can remember seeing. An alternative to this is to remove one or more items after the first look, then allow a minute's observation, and the child has to name those items that have been removed.

GAMES TO AID SELF-CARE TASKS

DRESSING

Play dressing-up games using a variety of dressing-up clothes and a big dice. Place pictures of the clothes on each side of the dice. The child has to roll the dice and then find the matching piece of clothing. After five goes the child has to dress in the clothes he has won. He needs to put the clothes on in the correct order.

TOILETING

These games help to improve balance and help children to reach round their bodies to aid bottom-wiping. The children stand in long rows and have to pass a ball between their legs to the next person in the row. They continue to the end and then the last person comes to the front of the row and starts again. This could be done as a relay race.

Another game is to get the child to place his hands behind his back and put an object in his hands. He has to describe what he can feel while the other children have to guess what it is.

BODY PARTS

Ask one child to lie on a big sheet of paper while another child draws around him. Get the child to complete the picture adding in different body parts – nose, mouth, hair, toes and fingers.

Children with DCD sometimes have additional difficulties with attention and concentration. Activities to promote good listening skills will help the child, and games such as Simon Says, where the child has to listen to commands, are excellent.

Substitute 'Simon' with 'teacher': 'Teacher says place your right hand on your right hip.'

Other listening games include musical chairs, where the children move in and around the chairs. The child has to listen and to respond to the music stopping. You could also put together a sound game with different sounds the child has to recognize, such as animal noises or familiar household noises like a bath running, the television, a dog barking. This could be linked to pictures of the sounds and the child could play a version of Lotto and match the sound to the picture.

Hunt the sound is a good game too. Blindfold the child and play different sounds. The child then has to tell which direction they are coming from. If you introduce a number of sounds he then has to listen for the order of the sounds.

Create some 'noisemakers' with the children by putting dried rice, macaroni, peas or beads into empty plastic juice bottles and screwing the lid on. Then get the children to 'play' them in a band. This teaches them to take turns and listen for when they need to join in.

BETTER LISTENING SKILLS

IDEA

61

The more the child can practise strategies to aid concentration and attention the more he will be able to take part in activities in the classroom and avoid being distracted.

These suggestions help the child to build up his ability to attend and concentrate.

Place two or three objects in front of the child and ask him to point to one object, then two and three, for example, a car, a doll, a cup. Move the objects further away so he has further to reach and more time to remember the commands. Increase the complexity of the commands, for example, 'Put the doll on the car', 'Place the doll on her front and the cup behind the car'.

A second idea could be to give the child some action commands. These could be done beside a desk in a classroom, for example, 'Touch your toes'. Increase the complexity of the commands by lengthening the instructions. Even harder for the child is to put a time delay in between you giving the command and the child carrying out the action, for example, 'Start touching your toes and turning around three times when you hear the bell.'

Another suggestion is to tell the child a short story in simple sentences and ask him to repeat it to you. Playing games such as 'shop' and gradually increasing the number of items he needs to remember, for example, 'I went to the shops and I bought an orange, an apple and a pair of shoes' will also improve concentration. The child has to sit and attend to be able to participate.

With any activity, adding a 'doing' element increases the interest level for the child. For example, have a board with different coloured pegs and tell the child to place the pegs in different arrangements increasing in complexity once each stage is achieved – a) place three blue pegs along, b) place two blue pegs along and one red peg down, and so on.

The dyspraxic child often needs to see what his strengths are, so playing games where he can see that other children have strengths and weaknesses and likes and dislikes, can help boost his self-esteem. Other children in the class also become aware of the differences between all of us, as well as the similarities.

Get all the children in a circle and go around the circle playing the 'favourites' game. 'What is your favourite . . . food, TV programme, game to play, piece of music or song.' 'What makes you happiest or saddest?' 'What animal do you like the most?' 'If you could go anywhere in the world where would it be and why?' 'What is your favourite colour?' Their answers could be quite revealing.

Alternatively, go around the circle and ask each child to say something positive about the person sitting next to them. Try getting the children to dream about their futures.

Use open questions such as, 'Where would you like to live?' 'Who would live with you?' 'What type of work would you do?' 'Where would you go on holiday?'

When you come to do an activity in class, try grouping the children into the months they were born in or by their favourite colour. It offers an opportunity for children to interact with different children in the class.

RAISING SELF-ESTEEM

IDEA 63

Some children with DCD may not like certain touch sensations and find it hard to detect the differences between various textures. Try to find activities where they can get used to handling different substances and feeling and experiencing different textures.

This is fun to do and children will love it. First make the Sticky Stuff using the recipe below, then create a number of different textures to work with.

Recipe for Sticky Stuff:

2 packets of cornflour
2 cups of water
Food colouring
Large container

Mix the water and the cornflour to a thick consistency. The child could do this task as well. Get him to put his hands in and talk about the texture, the temperature, and the consistency. Make patterns on a plastic mat with it. Get the child to use the end of a paintbrush first and then his fingers to create different patterns.

You could also get together a variety of food with different textures, such as cooked spaghetti, different pasta shapes, cooked and uncooked rice, and discuss how these feel. Get the child to make a collage using them. You could do the same with textured materials, including velvet, card, corrugated paper, braid, lace, cotton material and foam. Use these also to make textured rubbings with a thick crayon. To do this select a few textured materials and place paper over their surface. Rub the crayon over the paper.

Secondary school

MOVING TO A BIGGER SCHOOL

Orientation around a new school may be difficult for young people with DCD, especially if they are moving from a smaller primary school to a much larger secondary school. They will benefit from having as much information as possible and becoming as familiar as practicable with their new environment as early as they can.

Try to arrange for visits to the school on several occasions in the final two terms before the move and have a link person the young person can relate to. This could be an older pupil or the SENCO in the school.

Take photos of the school and create a school map. This task could be undertaken by older pupils as a group project. Place copies of the map in several prominent places around the school. A smaller version could be produced and given to all pupils before starting at the school.

There will probably be also a bewildering number of new faces to get used to. Digital photos of key teachers could be photocopied and given to new pupils so they have a chance of putting names to faces. Get pupils to wear stickers with their names on them for the first few weeks, if possible, to aid memory and increase the chances of making friends.

The pupil with DCD may not be streetwise with regards to 'how' to wear his uniform to blend in with the other students. Get older pupils to create their own rule book to pass on to the pupil and others who may have difficulties. Being aware of some of these unwritten and subtle 'rules' may give him a head start in the friendship stakes. For example, sometimes the way young people wear their shoes can be a trend, such as laces tucked in, also the type of bag used to carry books, and current hairstyles. All these subtleties can mark out the pupil as different from or more similar to their peers. Young people with DCD may not be good at picking out these more subtle social cues which can ease their transition into the new surroundings.

When arriving at a new school it is sometimes easier to get to know the 'real rules' such as 'don't run in the corridor' than the 'non-rules'. The 'non-rules' are the sort of rules that may vary from class to class and in different settings. For example, at lunchtimes in the canteen, should you queue or not, keep your plate on the tray or take it off?

Get together with a few teachers and run through what the potential 'non-rules' may be for different settings. Imagine you were landing from another planet and you had not learnt the social rules for that school. This can be similar for children coming from another country where, for example, greeting one another may be done in a different way.

Examples of areas to consider where rules may vary include:

○ In assembly – discuss the procedure for entering and leaving. Tell the pupil what he needs to do, such as waiting until others stand before he gets up.
○ In science – explain when you have to stand or sit.
○ Going to the toilet – discuss the protocol for asking.
○ Addressing different members of staff – discuss what is expected.

Look at your school rules and think about whether they are really clear and cannot be misinterpreted, for example, 'be kind' – this could be interpreted by different pupils in different ways because of their own experiences. Make a list of rules and consequences and post them up in key places around the school. Make these as visual as possible, rather than just a list of words.

TRAVELLING TO SCHOOL

Starting secondary school may be the first time a young person has travelled alone. There may be difficulties with:

o getting on the right bus
o getting to the bus on time
o managing money or the bus pass, especially if there is a queue of other young people
o who to sit next to on the bus.

Discuss with the pupil how he could use a bus pass, and encourage a dry run with parents before the start of term. It can be useful to assign an older student as a buddy to accompany the pupil on the journey to start with, until he is used to it or has made other friends. It is helpful if the pupil knows where to sit and with whom they are sitting – often there is a hierarchy of who sits where, informally kept to by the pupils, so try and get some feeling for this.

If the pupil walks to school, discuss how he can use buildings and other landmarks such as parks and crossings as route markers until he is familiar with the journey.

The pupil with DCD often finds it harder to navigate his way around new surroundings. He may have come from a small primary school which he knows well to a large secondary school where it may seem daunting to negotiate getting from class to class. Changing classrooms and having different teachers for different lessons can make it very stressful and increase the likelihood of losing possessions and not having the right equipment for the right class.

Provide a consistent colour-coding system in the school to include not only books and timetables (see Idea 69) but also, for example, coloured strips which could be painted on the steps of buildings, or plastic strips on doors to signify different lessons – biology in green and English in yellow. Make sure that all classrooms are clearly labelled and have arrows leading to class areas. Older pupils in the school can be appointed as buddies for the first week in break and lunchtimes.

GETTING AROUND SCHOOL

PERSONAL POSSESSIONS

Carrying possessions around a large school can mean that the young person with DCD can lose books, pens and equipment all over the school.

If you have lockers in your school, allow the individual to have one centrally located so that he can easily return to get books between classes. Make sure that you have spare locker keys or know the combination numbers as the pupil is more likely to lose keys than his peers. If you do not have any lockers, consider setting up a few centrally to help some young people who present with these difficulties. Imagine having to carry all your books and equipment around, and possibly even a laptop as well, all day, every day!

The young person should have all his possessions clearly labelled, including his pencil case and rucksack/bag and all sports clothes and shoes. Have a clear policy for lost property so the pupil knows where to go if he has lost his possessions.

Starting a new school can be daunting, and so too can a new school year when the curriculum changes completely. Knowing where to go and when is important. Young people with DCD commonly have difficulties with organization. Moving around a school carrying books and equipment can be difficult to do, especially if there is nowhere such as a locker or desk to leave books and equipment between lessons.

Colour-coding the timetable will be a big help. A specific colour can be used for each subject and this can correspond with the folders or exercise books. When the young person looks at his timetable the colour alone helps to prompt him to see which subject he has next. Make several copies of the timetable so that he can put one copy up on the wall of his bedroom, one in the kitchen at home, one in a locker (if he has one) and one on the inside of his homework book. If the timetable changes, be sure to let him know.

It can be useful to discuss with the individual what equipment they may need for each class and get them to write this down until it becomes automatic for them.

THE TIMETABLE

COMMUNICATION BETWEEN TEACHERS

Communication in a large secondary school can be a challenge. Some teachers will only work with some pupils for one or two classes per week, which can result in it taking some time for the teacher to get used to how specific children learn and where their difficulties may lie.

Sharing information is essential to ensure that the young person is supported as well as possible. A liaison diary or 'passport' can be one way of ensuring this – the pupil can carry this and it may well help communication between home and school, as well as within school itself. The pupil could create his own passport. Ask him to glue his photograph to a note card or an index card and then encourage him to add personalized information, such as interests and goals, likes and dislikes, family members and special friends. Some of this information could also be shared with the class.

The SENCO might be willing to coordinate the passport and encourage all teachers to write on it what has worked well to support the pupil and also where things have not gone so well. This can be extremely helpful in determining the best approach for each individual.

If the school has an intranet system, use this as a method of alerting other teachers when any problems arise. Also encourage the learning support assistants to pass on positive information if they are working with the pupil and recognize an approach that works well for him.

Liaison between home and school is often much harder to undertake once the young person moves from primary to secondary school. The more casual contact and brief conversations between staff and parents don't occur in the same way, because usually the young person comes alone to school or gets dropped off.

If possible, arrange a meeting before the start of term and introduce the person who can be the named link at the school, thereby reducing parental anxiety and promoting a good working partnership.

Alternatively, set up a meeting with parents at the start of term and find out from the parents' perspective what worked and what did not in the previous school. It can make an enormous difference if you can start off 'on the right foot' and give the pupil confidence. The parent or guardian should be given a copy of the timetable, if available, and it is a good idea to show them around the school. Young people with DCD often lose possessions, but if parents know the layout they can talk their child through where they have been on that day and try and help them.

All parents should be aware of the school rules and the consequences of breaking them, so that they can reinforce these at home with their child.

If possible, every Friday during the year, send home a note describing the next week's schedule. This can include special events, birthdays, tests, quizzes, important assignments, trips, parents' nights, and assemblies.

HOME–SCHOOL LIAISON

IDEA

72

TOILETS

Toilets can remain a challenge in the secondary years. This may be due to difficulties negotiating new fastenings on trousers, and planning the sequence of necessary actions. Memory of a previous accident may result in the pupil avoiding going to the toilet all day and even limiting his fluid intake.

For both girls and boys, fastenings on clothes should not be tricky to open. Using Velcro in place of button or zip fastenings, especially in cuffs and at collars, or for tops of trousers, is a good idea. Some boys may find urinating without pulling trousers down difficult to do and this may result in them standing and exposing all! This difficulty will require sensitive handling. Some toilets in secondary school have limited access to toilet paper, so it can be helpful to have a small pack of wet wipes available.

Secondary school is a time of passing through puberty and beyond, and for girls with DCD who are starting their periods it may be doubly challenging. A lack of awareness of what is socially appropriate may result in the young person declaring their difficulties and not seeing the impact on potential peer relationships. Poor time concepts may lead to her being unaware of the need to change sanitary pads, resulting in accidents. Use a timer on a watch to remind the young girl, or encourage her to change the pads every breaktime. The actual process of changing pads may be harder to do, so check with the mother if this could be a potential problem. Poor organizational skills may also result in forgotten sanitary pads – having a spare pack (as well as spare knickers) somewhere pre-arranged will be helpful in emergencies.

Sensitive liaison between mother and teacher can generally overcome great embarrassment and reduce the risk of unwanted accidents.

There is evidence that young people with DCD have fewer friends and have difficulty in social situations. The gap between them and their peers often opens up at this stage, as the young person is not so good at picking up the 'nods and grunts' of non-verbal communication which make up so much of normal social interaction.

Consider opportunities for the pupil to share his interests and be seen as a valued class member. A hobbies session where everyone talks about their hobbies or interests is one way of encouraging this.

Mentor systems which have older pupils helping to guide the young person can be useful, or you could consider setting up a group at lunchtimes to help improve skills. This could be for 'shy' young people, as well as those with some difficulties. During discussions, find out what the main topics of conversation in the playground are. Additional information, such as what films others are watching, what music they listen to, what is popular to wear, would also be useful to know. This could also be undertaken as a form or group project and used by other new pupils coming into the school, as well as the young person with DCD.

Role-play is a good way of practising skills such as starting or breaking off a conversation and greeting people. This could be introduced into PSHE classes. Recording and playing back these sessions can help the pupils to see where areas can be improved. A secondary school version of circle time, where pupils share ideas and all have an opportunity to turn-take and be listened to, can also be helpful.

Another idea to encourage turn-taking and participation is to write each pupil's name on a craft stick. Store the sticks in an unbreakable container and use them to call on pupils during class activities and discussions and make sure everyone gets a turn. The sticks can also be used to pick partners or groups for cooperative activities.

MAKING FRIENDS

IDEA

74

Most teenagers want to push the boundaries and see how far they can go. This is a normal part of adolescence, but the young person with DCD may be later at starting this behaviour and may come across as more cautious than his peers. However, peer pressure may result in him taking risks without understanding the potential consequences because of his need to gain peer recognition.

Circle time or PSHE lessons in school provide opportunities to talk through strategies such as learning to say 'no' and how to ask for help. Opportunities for positive social success are essential, and drama groups can also be a way of exploring how different and similar all young people are.

Where possible, the young person should be given some responsibility so that others can witness his potential. Make sure that he is successful and this is visible to others. Clubs where activities are not all team based – crafts such as pottery and photography, or sports such as swimming, badminton and martial arts or going to the gym – can be an excellent way for the pupil with DCD to gain peer recognition.

Try games that promote interaction, such as Chat Back. This is a knockout competition, played in pairs. Each person has to keep talking at the other person. It does not matter what they are talking about, but there must be no repetition or pauses. You will need a referee to decide the winner of each pair.

It is important to remember that although the child with DCD may be of secondary school age, he may still have social skills set more at a primary school level. These classroom activities can be fun for all ages. When putting young people into pairs, try to pair more socially competent pupils with those with less developed skills.

Pair up pupils and give them identical sets of Lego or play dough. Put a cardboard screen between the Lego or the play dough so that one pupil cannot see the other. Ask one pupil to make a structure and when this is completed, ask the other one to make the same thing without looking at the other person's design but by following instructions. Requesting and receiving help teaches the pupils how to ask questions, listen and take turns in conversation. This activity is a great one for demonstrating the need for clear communication and checking instructions.

Twenty Questions – create a file of pictures from magazines and ask a pupil to select a picture from it of a 'secret object'. The other children then have 20 'yes or no' questions in order to guess what the object is. Objects can be from a subject area, for example, geography, to add an additional learning element to the task.

Blindfold maze drawing – pupils work in pairs and are given a drawn maze to complete. One pupil is blindfolded and the other is asked to give directions that help the blindfolded pupil move his/her pencil through the maze. Alternatively, try making a maze out of masking tape on the floor and getting a friend to physically lead the pupil through the maze. You can change this game by building an obstacle course. The game allows pupils to be helped by each other and emphasizes the importance of trust in friendships. It can also teach other pupils what it is like to have difficulties such as being visually impaired, and can be a way into other discussions about disability and differences.

Young people with DCD may show what appears to be disruptive and negative behaviour. This may be a sign of frustration at not getting the full picture and failing to understand the nuances of language.

Record where this is happening and when. It may be happening in lessons where more complex language is being used, such as mathematics, or in a language class such as French. If this is the case have a further look to see where the understanding is breaking down. Also note down what behaviour is seen – is the young person remorseful? Young people with DCD are not commonly oppositional and usually want to apologize after the event. However, they may not know why the incident happened. You need to work with them to get them to recognize that the behaviour is not acceptable, even though the reasons for feeling negative may have been.

When instructions are given they should be clear and you need to check for understanding – a nod may not mean the young person has understood. It's useful to write down the instructions as well as saying them. If there is negative behaviour, make sure the rules and consequences are clear and unambiguous. Talk through what has happened and ask the young person how he thinks it could be avoided next time.

Consider where his difficulties lie and whether adaptations or adjustments can be put in place to help reduce feelings of frustration.

Young people with DCD may feel more anxious in new or changing situations. Understanding what and when things are happening can help to reduce anxiety.

Talk with the young person about what may make them anxious. Examination times for all pupils are often stressful, but especially so if writing, organizing thoughts and getting them down on paper are difficult. Also, he may have experienced less success at examinations, performing usually better in class.

The pupil needs to be taught strategies for coping with stress. Relaxation techniques – counting to ten and learning to go through a relaxation routine – can be very helpful. There are a number of relaxation CDs available, such as *Complete Relaxation* by Glenn Harrold. If possible, create a quiet place in school where the pupil can go at breaktimes if he is feeling anxious. Sometimes playing music can be calming or may aid concentration – if he has a laptop, music could be listened to (by prior agreement) while working on other studies. He may need to listen to different types of music to find out which works best.

REDUCING STRESS AND ANXIETY

The young person with DCD is likely to continue to have handwriting difficulties into secondary school and may be much better at expressing himself verbally. He may be at a disadvantage academically if he has to write by hand during examinations.

An amanuensis may make all the difference to passing well or failing an exam badly. However, using a scribe and telling someone else what to write is a skill that needs to be practised before the examination.

If additional time in examinations is going to be provided, it will need to be decided some time in advance. Young people with DCD may need more help with getting their ideas down on paper, and practising examination techniques early and embedding them so they become automatic is important.

It's vital also to work with the pupil to create a study timetable so he can see what he needs to do and in what time frame, as time concepts may be very poor. During the examination itself, a watch with a vibrating alarm that can be set to vibrate at certain times can be helpful to prompt the pupil to move on. It is quite common to see some pupils not realizing how much time has gone and completing a great first question on a paper but never getting to the second question as they have run out of time.

The pupil may be more fidgety than his peers and this may be due to difficulties maintaining postural balance and also trying to maintain attention.

Try to reduce distractions by positioning the pupil facing the front of the class where possible. Consider the class layout and make sure he is in the most stable position in order to do the tasks being asked of him. For example, in science, standing to undertake experiments may be better than sitting on a stool with legs dangling down. You may see the young person constantly moving and readjusting his position in order to become balanced.

Try using a seating wedge to 'tilt' the young person into a more stable position. Seating wedges can be obtained from a number of sources, such as Back in Action (www.backinaction.co.uk). Check to see if he has his feet on the floor as a means to improve stability. If he just has to fidget, give him a fiddle toy such as Blu-Tak or a soft ball.

CLASSROOM LAYOUT

WRITING SKILLS

If writing remains a problem at the age of 11 it is unlikely to improve significantly. The young person may find it harder to record information at speed, copy information from the board and write neatly so that others can read it. This means that writing is often slower and more laborious. For pupils in secondary school the demand for recording increases, and if the effort is too much then the pupil with DCD may produce shorter pieces of work or become increasingly frustrated by the look and quality of his work.

The amount of written work can be limited by providing photocopied worksheets. The sheets can then be glued into workbooks or put into plastic pockets so that they do not get in a muddle. Try to limit the quantity of work that needs to be copied from the board, and work on alternative means of recording. Unless a particular topic really requires handwriting, a computer could be used and this may encourage greater creativity. The young person could build up a list of common words he needs to write and spell and these could be available as a word bank to use either manually or on the laptop. Remember when marking to mark the content of work and not the neatness if possible.

While the computer is an excellent tool for writing, encourage the pupil to practise a consistent signature. This may be important for positive self-esteem and is worth devoting time to.

If the pupil has difficulties with writing, an alternative means of recording information could be a word processor, a portable palm pilot, a laptop or desktop computer. There is a lot of choice available.

The Dana Alpha Smart is a portable keyboard and word processor. The advantage of this product is that it is light, has a long battery life and is a cheaper alternative to a laptop. It is slim to carry so it can fit into a school bag or rucksack. However, the screen is smaller than a laptop.

A pocket PC offers portability and battery length and can be used with a keyboard either connected to the pocket PC or palm pilot. Alternatively there are wireless versions. It is light and easy to use, but again has a small screen.

A laptop will have a decent sized screen and usually a larger keyboard. Battery life may not be as good as a Dana Alpha Smart. As not all laptops are light, this additional weight for the young person, who is carrying all his books and paraphernalia around, could be problematic. Make sure there is access to a plug where the pupil can recharge the laptop battery. Consider how work will be printed off from the laptop and arrange access to a printer.

Security is always a concern and it's useful if there are lockers available for depositing expensive equipment at break and lunchtimes. Insurance for a laptop is essential, as it could be dropped or knocked or even stolen.

RECORDING INFORMATION

IDEA

82

Organizational difficulties often result in poor time management. The pupil often has poor time concepts and may be unaware when to move on to another piece of work. Keeping to time in an examination and pacing himself appropriately can also be problematic. The pupil may require external reminders of time moving on. Suggest that he wears a watch with an alarm. Some watches are available that vibrate rather than ring and so would not interrupt others around him.

Suggest also using a kitchen timer and give him a set amount of time in which to complete a piece of work. The timer may need to be out of vision because this in itself may be a distraction. Using a timer will allow the young person to gradually build up concepts of what certain periods of time are. Try relating time to activities the pupil does on a regular basis, for example, if it takes ten minutes to walk to school talk about this so he can think about what this feels like. He will probably have a time of day when he works better, so find out when this is and discuss how he can work at these times.

Analogue clocks are sometimes better to use than digital, as they enable the pupil to see time passing.

It's important to start typing skills as early as possible. *Typequick* is a fun program with games that the younger age child will enjoy, and *Typing Instructor Deluxe* is a good program for all ages in secondary school, with subject-specific areas as well as general areas reinforcing spelling.

Use autotext in Microsoft *Word* and put in commonly used words. This program has word prediction software built in and can speed up typing and reduce spelling errors.

It's also worth considering text-to-speech software if the pupil makes errors when recording but does not see them. This allows the young person to hear what he has written. *Claroread* and *Texthelp Read and Write Gold* are programs that allow text to be read aloud to the student.

Speech-to-text software can also be useful. There are a number of programs such as *Dragon Dictate* that only need an hour or two for the pupil to be able to use them competently. However, if the young person has unclear speech or his voice is breaking or changing markedly it is best to leave this for when he's a little older.

IDEA 84

Getting homework down at the end of the lesson may be difficult to do if writing is slow and the pupil is worrying about getting to the next lesson.

Write homework on the whiteboard so that the pupil has time to copy it down during the lesson and is not in a rush at the end of it. Another idea is to print out labels with the homework written on and every pupil can just 'peel' them off and place them in their homework diary.

A buddy system can also work well with homework problems. The buddy could record the information and then either photocopy it or use carbon paper underneath his/her work to provide a copy for the pupil with DCD. Alternatively, the buddy could send an email about the homework to the pupil's own email address. Often young people with DCD do not have the same network of friends and as a result do not have the ability to 'just make a call' or go on MSN for a chat – this may need to be more formally done.

The school's intranet could have a homework site so that pupils can access this after their lesson, or you could consider setting up an answering machine as a homework hotline. Your pupils would have no more excuses for missed assignments!

A dictaphone can be a useful device for recording homework – mini voice recorders are available from Boots, for example.

Young people with DCD often have difficulty planning work, and getting off the starting blocks to write an essay can be onerous. In addition, planning how long each piece of work is likely to take and how much to write for each part of an essay may be difficult.

It can help to create essay templates so that the pupil knows how to fit information in and can see what is expected of him. Allowing him to have a look at examples of other pupils' previous work will also give him an idea of the style expected.

Work out a timetable for the pupil so he knows when he has to complete the task, and use a timer with him so he gets used to knowing when to move on to the next section or question. Teach alternative note-taking strategies to get ideas down on paper, such as concept mapping or making bullet points first before writing out the essay or assignment.

Editing skills are important too, so encourage him to check for errors in spelling, punctuation, correct headings and so on.

Set up a system to evaluate how well the pupil is doing, but use self-evaluation. For example, I sit all my letters on the line 'all of the time', 'most of the time', 'some of the time', 'none of the time'. Ask the young person what he needs to work on, so that he can identify areas of weakness for himself.

ESSAY WRITING

CONCEPT MAPPING ON PAPER

The pupil is likely to have come across concept mapping at primary school (see Idea 35). Build on skills learnt or teach them if they are not in place.

Reinforce the different phases:

○ A brainstorming phase – put down ideas on Post-it® notes.

○ An organizing phase – arrange them into groups.

○ A layout phase – arrange them into groups best representing the pupil's understanding of the inter-relationships and connections between groupings.

○ The linking phase – show the pupil how to use lines with arrows to connect and show the relationship between linked items. Write a word or short phrase by each arrow to show the relationship.

Show the pupil how he can add in simple pictures or symbols to reinforce the groupings. He could also use different colours to highlight the different areas.

For the young person with DCD whose writing and drawing limits a paper-based approach there are some excellent concept mapping computer programs. Some of these, such as *Inspiration* and the more junior version of *Kidspiration*, have a range of visual icons related to subject areas.

Mind-mapping can be a good way of 'dumping' ideas first, before going on to concept mapping. *Stick-Up* is one program that can be used in this way and the pupil can then re-arrange the ideas and colour coordinate them into themes. It has a simple essay template.

MindManager, *Ygnius* and *Mindfull* are also computer-based concept mapping programs. Each one has a different style. Many can be trialled free for 30 days, enabling the pupil to play with the software and see what best suits him. *Mindfull*, for example, allows the user to record ideas as well as show visual representations. Concept maps produced in *Mindfull* can be sent to a *Word* program, or to *PowerPoint*. This program allows the user to import their photos as well.

CONCEPT MAPPING USING SOFTWARE

MATHEMATICS AND TOOLS

Tools where good coordination is required are harder to manipulate. An alternative to using a protractor and pair of compasses is a circle scribe, which is a round flat disc that can be used as a pair of compasses but is easier to manoeuvre (see www.circlescribe.co.uk).

A ruler with a ridge or something to hold on to may be easier to handle than a flat one. As an alternative to using a ridged ruler, try screwing a small door knob into a wooden ruler so that the pupil can hold onto this. Putting a small piece of non-stick matting on the end of the ruler can help stop it moving around when drawing lines. Alternatively, the pupil may find an architect's roller ruler is easier to use as these glide across the page and stay in one plane.

Consider using lined paper or paper with larger squares as it may be easier to use than small squares if writing is poor and the pupil has difficulties copying from the board. It is also a good idea to provide stencils for shapes used in mathematics and science, rather than expecting the pupil to draw them himself.

Number concepts may remain poor as the child moves into secondary school. There may be two explanations for this: there are sometimes visual perceptual difficulties where the young person may not be able to visualize what numbers look like, or there can be difficulties with the language of mathematics.

The young person needs to see geometric shapes as real shapes rather than as pictures on a page. Cut out shapes and allow the pupil actually to manipulate them.

He may find it hard copying figures from the board and make errors during this process, resulting in getting answers wrong, even if he has understood the concepts. Having the textbook beside him so that he can copy figures directly will help, or use photocopied sheets to limit recording errors. Checking understanding of mathematical terms may also help, and try to use consistent language – for example, don't vary the use of plus, and, add, addition for '+'. Make some cards for each symbol and show the alternative names for that symbol. These could be posted around the walls of the classroom to remind all the pupils.

If times tables remain a difficulty, use visual means to learn them and show how the numbers build up, as well as looking at software programs like *Numbershark* (see Idea 39).

A good website for mathematics is www.amt.org.uk which shows a Slavonic abacus that can be used to illustrate number concepts. Also worth a visit is www.bbc.co.uk/schools/numbertime/

MANAGING MATHEMATICAL CONCEPTS

COOKERY AND CDT LESSONS

Encouraging independent living skills will help the pupil with DCD to gain confidence and prepare for the next stage of life.

Before the lesson, consider undertaking a risk assessment to check if there is a requirement for additional monitoring when using knives and other equipment. Assess the equipment too. Rubber handles on kitchen implements will make them easier to grip.

Guide the young person to cut or stir from a standing position as this will create more stability than sitting on a stool with legs dangling down. A rubber mat such as Dycem can reduce movement of cups and beakers, making it easier to pour items and stir. It's also a good idea to use a timer to get the child to become aware of planning, preparation and cooking time.

For CDT and craft work, specialist scissors such as craft scissors from Peta can be used and are easier to manipulate with one hand if complex shapes need to be cut.

You could get an older group of pupils to prepare this for younger pupils, or do it with the pupil with DCD. This is a great group activity as different members of the class could be in charge of different aspects of the project, such as photography or design.

Packed full of delicious recipes, the visual cookery book will help the young person with DCD see exactly what items of equipment are required and he can follow each stage by looking at the pictures rather than just having to read the words. It allows the pupil to 'see' all the steps.

First decide which recipes are going to be included. To start with keep this simple, with things such as beans on toast or making a cake. Talk to the young person about what ingredients you may need, get these out and take a digital photo of each ingredient.

Then get out the utensils required and take photos of each of these. Put all of these into a book in order with pictures of the actual steps such as mixing and pouring.

Have a picture of the oven or cooker showing the temperature required and a picture of the clock showing how long it will take. Laminate all the pictures to prevent spills from ruining the recipe book, or put them in plastic pockets. All the recipes could then be put into an A4 folder with a plastic cover.

A VISUAL COOKERY BOOK

IDEA 92

Mathematics is often a big problem for the young person with DCD. Cookery can be a great time to reinforce many of the concepts that may be causing confusion.

Introduce the concepts of weights and measures and discuss these when weighing out ingredients. You could also talk about geometric shapes by cutting up a cake or using a cutter to create different shapes in pastry.

Different recipes can illustrate different scientific principles, for example, applying heat to ingredients changes their chemical structure, adding water changes the consistency.

The following recipe can be used to discuss mathematics and science concepts. Try making sherbet. There are only three ingredients and no cooking involved.

○ Sugar, usually caster or icing sugar
○ Bicarbonate of soda
○ Powdered or crystalline citric acid.

Measure out two teaspoons of sugar, one teaspoon of citric acid and half a teaspoon of bicarbonate of soda. Mix together. Make sure the equipment and ingredients are dry (this is really important).

Flavourings can be added to this. Provide the pupils with something to dip into the sherbet and let them taste it – they will get a fizzy feeling on their tongues, caused by a chemical reaction between the citric acid and the bicarbonate of soda.

COOKERY WITH MATHEMATICS AND SCIENCE

Playing in a team is often very difficult for the young person with DCD. On arriving at secondary school they may still not have the prerequisite skills to be competent at playing football, netball or rugby, for example, and may need continuing help and support if they are to play these games.

Do not assume that the young person knows the rules of the game he is playing – they will need to be explained clearly and you should check for understanding.

'Talk back' is a useful technique used in supporting young people with DCD. Break down the skills and practise them, ask him to say how the skill could be improved and what he thinks he needs to do. Guided coaching will help the young person first visualize the task and then talking through what he needs to do will reinforce this.

Place younger pupils in smaller groups – put stronger with weaker players at times. When catching, throwing or kicking are involved the stronger player has a greater range of balls to try to catch, throw or kick and this also allows the weaker player to partner someone who can kick or throw more accurately.

PREPARING FOR TEAM GAMES

GRADING THE ACTIVITY

To ensure success with ball games, it is best to introduce them by first grading the activity. For example, when introducing badminton skills, first try to play 'no net' badminton. This is basically a game without the net, but allows for a greater chance of success. 'Slams' are not allowed and the shuttle must always be hit up, but otherwise all other rules apply.

Another indoor wet weather activity is balloon volleyball. This allows the pupil with DCD to participate as the slow movement of the balloon gives players a chance to move into the correct position and catch it. Adding a second or third balloon can increase the difficulty level for the teams.

No-rules basketball is another way of introducing basketball and giving the pupil with DCD a chance to participate and have fun. Choose one team to start from the back of the court. The players are allowed to dribble, walk or run with the ball, and can take as long as they want to get to the other end of the court. The other team can only obtain the ball if it is dropped or they intercept a pass. A successful shot scores two points.

Being last to be chosen or having your peers say they don't want you in their team at all can leave a scar on any young person's landscape of confidence. Avoiding these scenes and encouraging positive opportunities for successful participation are important.

Allow the pupil to be the one to choose the team some of the time, or choose the teams yourself instead. Alternatively, put names in a hat and randomly draw them out or use a pack of cards and give out sets of hearts and diamonds to get pupils into teams.

Consider having an 'all-comers' team as well as the elite teams in the school. Some young people with DCD may want to play netball or football, for example, but never get the opportunity to play in a team because their peers are better than they are.

CHOOSING TEAMS

Complex games or sports skills need to be broken down into component tasks and you should teach these first. Explain how to complete an activity/action, and give a demonstration if necessary. Allow the young person to participate partially at first, for example, let them just bowl in cricket, then be the scorer.

Some allowance may need to be made in the rules of the game while the pupil is becoming proficient. By providing support and encouragement he will gain positive experiences in physical activities and this will help him enjoy them more, as well as improving his level of general fitness. Where the activity seems too difficult or the pupil becomes discouraged, give him a less active role such as scorer or umpire.

Less competitive sports or activities where the young person only has to measure his skills against his own performance, such as golf, archery and snooker, can also be good alternatives. Circuit training can also be a satisfying alternative to contact or ball sports.

The young person may enjoy games that work in teams and require group participation but do not highlight an individual's skills. For example, try playing Soccer Ball. Divide players into two sides: attackers and defenders. Defenders form a circle 'fort', holding hands and facing outward, with their captain in the centre. Attackers surround the fort at about eight or ten paces away. They try to kick a soccer ball into the fort; it may go through the legs of the defenders or over their heads. If it goes over their heads, the captain may catch it and throw it out, but if it touches the ground inside the circle, the fort is captured and the players change sides.

It is important that young people with DCD are encouraged to participate in physical activity which will improve their coordination and their confidence, but it doesn't have to be a team-based game. After all, as adults we do not all play team games. Try some of these games:

○ Tri-golf – this golf game can be set up in a sports hall or in the playground and provides the basics of golf. It can be graded according to skill level, and can encourage group participation.

○ Swimming – lots of young people with DCD find swimming their most successful sporting activity. They may find doing lengths and swimming 'stylishly' harder to do, but being in the water and participating is great fun and should be encouraged.

○ Trampolining – this is a great sport for improving core stability and posture and can be undertaken in groups.

○ Yoga and martial arts – these promote body awareness, increase confidence and improve coordination.

○ Fencing and archery – these can improve shoulder stability and hand-to-eye coordination.

○ Badminton and horse riding – these are sports which young people with DCD can actively participate in and enjoy immensely.

NON-TEAM-BASED GAMES

PREPARING FOR TRANSITION –
INTERVIEWS AND CAREERS

Choosing the right career is hard for most of us, but for the young person with DCD it may be more difficult because of problems moving through education, and not having a clear sense of direction and purpose. He may even think that he needs to continue to use (in a workplace setting) his weakest skills. This may be because support in school has concentrated on his weaknesses and not always worked on enhancing his strengths. This approach may result in him making poor career choices as he may lack insight into what he could potentially do.

Talk to the pupil about his interests and hobbies as these may be the route to choosing a specific career. Focus on a strengths-based model and look for ways of supporting or avoiding weaknesses. It is reassuring at this stage to suggest he will be free to use a range of strategies in college and university that may not have been options while in school, for example, if handwriting is a difficulty he could try specific dictation software such as *Dragon Dictate*.

Discuss the issue of having to handwrite a covering letter with an application form, as his poor handwriting may be misjudged and the pupil deemed to be lacking the skills required. Encourage him to complete forms online where possible.

It's important to practise interview skills. This should include what to wear and how to sit, as scruffy attire, a slovenly posture, a weak handshake and poor eye contact may lead the interviewer to conclude that the individual is uninterested.

Moving from school to college provides a new setting, new course and new challenges.

Talk through what course the young person wants to do and consider carefully what aspects, if any, may require additional support. It is useful to compile a list of colleges and universities where you know the level of student support offered. Some may have more experience and interest in supporting young people with DCD, so it's worth contacting them to find out what they can provide.

You will need to ascertain what independent living skills the young person has and create a list of these. They may not bear any relationship to the young person's intelligence. See if the pupil has the skills to live away from home. Can he prepare meals, look after his clothing, shave, clean teeth, and manage money, for example? If independent living and social skills are not as good as his peers he will need to consider local options or take a 'gap year' to acquire them. If the pupil has difficulties orientating himself around new places, suggest it may be better for him to go to a town that is familiar to him or alternatively to make several visits to orientate himself before starting the course.

Help him to apply for a disabled student allowance (DSA) to make sure help and support is in place as early as possible. It is likely that if the young person has continuing motor difficulties he will have access to a computer and software to help, as well as a scribe for examinations and note-taking in lectures if required. Forms often have to be handwritten, so offer to complete these with him if this is a difficulty.

Many schools set up a mentoring scheme where one teacher is available to talk to and help with planning. Universities and colleges also have open days, so encourage the young person to attend. It's a good idea to find out if the college operates summer study skills sessions, as this would also be of help prior to starting on the course. Visit www.bild.org.uk for additional information.

ON TO COLLEGE OR UNIVERSITY

WORK EXPERIENCE

Work experience is important when helping the young person to decide what his future career may be. Poor work experiences may discourage the individual and can be potentially very damaging to their self-esteem and confidence.

Talk to the pupil about disclosing his difficulties during his placement and the advantages and disadvantages of doing so. He needs to think through what he is likely to have to do and consider where the 'hot spots' may be, for example, using a photocopier if organization is difficult, taking down telephone numbers accurately on the phone, meeting new people and greeting them, recording information in a meeting.

A new work environment provides new sets of rules, such as dress code, even rules regarding who should make the tea and how much time should be taken for lunch. Mentor the young person so he is able to ask about these rules. The employer may require to be told that the young person may require extra time to learn a new task and a bit longer than others to complete it.

USEFUL WEBSITES AND ORGANIZATIONS

○ www.dyspraxiafoundation.org.uk – a UK parent support organisation
○ www.dyscovery.co.uk – the Dyscovery Centre site has links to hundreds of other sites and a list of books and materials related to DCD and other specific learning difficulties
○ www.dyspraxia.org.nz – New Zealand parent support site
○ www.dyspraxiaireland.com – Irish support site
○ www.dfes.org.uk – Government educational site
○ www.becta.org.uk – British Educational Communications and Technology Agency
○ www.handwritinginterestgroup.org.uk– the UK Handwriting Special Interest Group
○ www.danda.org.uk – the adolescent and adult group for individuals with developmental disorders
○ www.golf-foundation.org – this organization stocks the tri-golf equipment and provides training and materials for schools
○ www.bbc.co.uk/keyskills/ – information and exercises on a wide range of topics, including ICT and communication.

USEFUL BOOKS

○ *Guide to Dyspraxia and Developmental Co-ordination Disorder* by Amanda Kirby (Souvenir Press)
○ *The Adolescent with Developmental Co-ordination Disorder* by Amanda Kirby (Jessica Kingsley Press)
○ *Introducing Mind Mapping to Children in 12 Easy Steps* by Eva Hoffman (Available from The Accelerated Learning Centre, Crown Buildings, Bancyfelin, Carmarthen SA33 5ND. www.accelerated-learning.co.uk)
○ *Learning Champs* by Colin Rose and Ann Civardi (Big Fish)

USEFUL SOFTWARE

○ *Mindfull, Inspiration* and *Kidspiration* – examples of concept mapping programs
○ *Stick-Up* – organizer software
○ *First Keys* – good program to allow the child to become keyboard aware
○ *Typequick* – great program with games to teach typing skills
○ *Typing Instructor Deluxe* – there are two versions of this program for primary and secondary school, both well received by children with DCD
○ www.dotolearn.com – this has free games and activities to download
○ www.mycorkboard.com – freely downloadable program called *Corkboard*, useful for daily organization. It has a 'to do' list, a timer, a digital or analogue clock and sits on the opening page of the computer.

ICT AND OTHER SPECIALIST SUPPLIERS

AVP
School Hill Centre, Chepstow, Monmouthshire NP16 5PH
Tel: 01291 625439
Email: sales@avp.co.uk
Website: www.avp.co.uk

REM
Great Western House, Langport, Somerset TA10 9YU
Tel: 01458 254700
Email: sales@r-e-m.co.uk
Website: www.r-e-m.co.uk

Iansyst
Fen House, Fen Road, Cambridge CB4 1UN
Tel: 01223 420101
Email: reception@dyslexic.com
Website: www.dyslexic.com
Provides specialist hard and software.

LDA
Tel: 0845 1204776
Website: www.ldalearning.com
Provides specialist equipment for the classroom
including scissors and pencil grips.

Inclusive Technology
Gatehead Business Park, Delph New Road, Delph,
Oldham OL3 5BX
Tel: 01457 819790
Email: inclusive@inclusive.co.uk
Website: www.inclusive.co.uk
Provides specialist hard and software.